D1112440

The E Generation

Prepared for the
Entrepreneurial Economy?

Marilyn L. Kourilsky • William B. Walstad

KENDALL/HUNT PUBLISHING COMPANY
4050 Westmark Drive   Dubuque, Iowa 52002

Copyright © 2000 by Kauffman Center for Entrepreneurial Leadership
at the Ewing Marion Kauffman Foundation

ISBN 0-7872-6892-5

Kendall/Hunt Publishing Company has the exclusive rights to reproduce this work,
to prepare derivative works from this work, to publicly distribute this work,
to publicly perform this work and to publicly display this work.

All rights reserved. No part of this publication may be reproduced,
stored in a retrieval system, or transmitted, in any form or by any
means, electronic, mechanical, photocopying, recording, or otherwise,
without the prior written permission of Kendall/Hunt Publishing Company.

Printed in the United States of America
10 9 8 7 6 5 4 3 2 1

DEDICATION

To Michie Slaughter, founding president of the Kauffman Center for Entrepreneurial Leadership at the Ewing Marion Kauffman Foundation and a champion of entrepreneurship education for youth and young adults.

CONTENTS

LIST OF TABLES

ACKNOWLEDGMENTS

The authors would like to thank Bob Rogers, who served as co-chairman of the national Marketable Skills Task Force of America's Promise—Alliance for Youth. His foresight regarding the importance of entrepreneurship and economics for enhancing the marketable skills of all youth inspired much of the research underlying this book. We also appreciate the contributions of Daniel Buchheit, Gary Heisserer, Greg Kourilsky, and Kurt Mueller, president of the Kauffman Center for Entrepreneurial Leadership. Their insights and suggestions helped to make this a better book. Special thanks also to Kelley Brine for his creative cartoons and to Kate Pope Hodel for managing the publication process, with assistance from Cindy White. Finally, we would like to acknowledge the support provided by the staff of the Gallup Organization and America's Promise.

FOREWORD

Having a chance to create and successfully operate your own venture is an integral aspect of the American dream. However, it's a dream that may never come true for succeeding generations if we, as a society, do not actively prepare our youth to think and act as entrepreneurs and intrapreneurs.

In this groundbreaking book, Drs. Marilyn Kourilsky and William Walstad boldly articulate the challenge and opportunity facing our nation's educators. Their research shows unequivocally that today's E (for "Entrepreneurial") Generation aspires to entrepreneurship, but is not being prepared to succeed. It's a dichotomy that leads to a disturbing question: Lacking an educational foundation and faith in their capabilities, how many will be willing to take the risks necessary for success?

America's youth are clearly calling on the educational system to prepare them to succeed in an economy that is becoming more entrepreneurial every day. "Raising the bar" by equipping all youth for entrepreneurship and entrepreneurial thinking would not only help those who do start their own businesses—but also those who ultimately decide to work for others. While the ability to recognize opportunities, take initiative, tolerate risk, and think and act independently are vital to the initiation of enterprises, these same characteristics will be increasingly expected of all members of the workforce.

The E Generation looks to the future by probing the readiness of today's youth and young adults, ages 14-30, to enter an evolving workplace. The authors then proceed to propose strategies for removing obstacles and facilitating success. Most importantly, this book addresses the proposition that in a very real sense, all young people who are unprepared for the entrepreneurial economy are "at risk."

Our hope at the Ewing Marion Kauffman Foundation is that *The E Generation* will serve as a catalyst for discussion, and ultimately for action leading to changes in our educational system. Only in this way can we ensure that America's young people are prepared to succeed and flourish in the entrepreneurial economy.

Louis W. Smith
President and Chief Executive Officer
Ewing Marion Kauffman Foundation
Kansas City, Missouri

Unprecedented Interest, Unlimited Potential

The startling results of more than half a dozen recent national studies tell the story: there is an unprecedented interest in entrepreneurship and the entrepreneurial process among the youth and young adults of our country. Of every 10 high school and college-age students, between six and seven of them aspire to start a business of their own. Moreover, this desire is unexpectedly context independent, spanning gender, ethnicity/race, and socioeconomic status.

Will these dreams be pursued to fruition or are they exercises in wishful thinking? When the "rubber" of aspiration meets the "road" of entrepreneurial venture initiation, who of this young vanguard will have the ability to recognize opportunities? Given a good idea, will they be able to develop it into a viable market initiative? Conversely, having recognized an opportunity, will they be able to generate ideas that effectively address it? What are the real and perceived obstacles they will face in the journey to achieve their visions? At the high school and college levels, in what roles and partnerships can education engage to help youth and young adults master these challenges?

As the entrepreneurial revolution of today accelerates, these are some of the key issues that must be addressed if our youth are to become the proactive innovators and effective participants that drive tomorrow's knowledge-based entrepreneurial economy.

The imposing accomplishments of start-up and rapidly growing small entrepreneurial ventures are accelerating their impressive challenge to the large corporation's once traditional domination of our economic destiny. The pattern of major corporate downsizings initiated in the 1980s—often linked to the new economic realities of international competition—was one of the key factors in this entrepreneurial transformation. It generated a large, disenfranchised pool of experienced managers and professionals who had ideas and energy—and were too young to retire.[1]

As the economic climate became more favorable for smaller firms, this pool of talent redirected its displaced energies to the viable career alternatives of initiating and growing creative ventures. In a classically contrarian counterpoint to the downsizing of large corporations, new business starts have been at an all-time high, and—propitiously—the number of new jobs generated by the growth of small business firms has dwarfed the number of the jobs eliminated by large firms.[2]

In the 21st century, we will increasingly rely on the lean and agile entrepreneurship of the small, growth-oriented business—rather than the resources, scale and market size of the large corporation—to fuel our economic growth through the creation of jobs and innovative goods and services. Now and for the foreseeable future, our economy appears destined to be driven increasingly by the forces and mindset of entrepreneurship and entrepreneurial thinking.

This trend is by no means limited to the traditional processes and resources that converge in a start-up business to produce new goods and services. Intrapreneurship—employee application of entrepreneurial thinking to the various internal functions of existing businesses—is emerging as an equally critical asset for business growth. Entrepreneurial teams within corporations and other types of organizations are now involved in all forms of creative ventures and operating functions. These teams must adapt quickly, creatively and successfully to a competitive environment with shifting global boundaries and a half-life for major change that is often measured in weeks.[3]

Given the current trends for start-ups and existing businesses, the 21st century will be dominated by the entrepreneur and by entrepreneurial thinking. The entrepreneur will create the new businesses that provide much of this country's innovation and new jobs, and that serve as a major source of economic growth. In addition, all people—not just those starting businesses—will need to be more entrepreneurial in whatever job or activity they undertake. In the 21st century, much of one's success in work and in life will be based on entrepreneurial thinking and actions.[4]

Generating Widespread Appeal

The entrepreneurial re-invention of the nation's economy is engaging almost every ethnic and socioeconomic segment of our society. Traditionally, entrepreneurship was the avenue for economic success for immigrants arriving in this nation. That trend still occurs on a regular basis as new immigrants from all nations of the world use their skills, energy, and imagination to improve their position in the U.S. economy.

Entrepreneurship is rapidly growing in favor among other major groups in our society. A telling signal of this appeal is the significant increase in the number of women who view entrepreneurship as a desirable career option. Women often have been lured to the self-determining potential of entrepreneurship out of frustration with what they perceived as corporate glass ceilings to advancement and inflexibility with respect to the balancing of work and family. Many of these ventures expanded from home-based businesses to much larger enterprises.[5]

Minority groups also are seeing the power of entrepreneurship to transform lives and communities. Over the past decade, the number of businesses owned by African-Americans increased by almost 50 percent. The number of firms owned by other minority groups, including those owned by Hispanics, Asian Americans and American Indians, has advanced by more than 80 percent.[6] These statistics reflect the sustained effort of minorities to participate fully in the entrepreneurial economy.

Defining the E Generation

Equally important for the nation's future is the already mentioned growing desire by youth to become part of the entrepre-

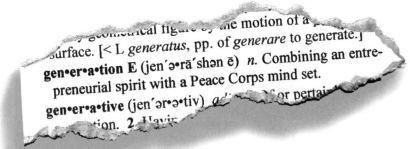

...cal fig... ...e motion of a ... surface. [< L *generatus*, pp. of *generare* to generate.] gen•er•a•tion E (jen´ə•rā´shən ē) *n.* Combining an entrepreneurial spirit with a Peace Corps mind set. gen•er•a•tive (jen´ər•ə•tiv) ... ...or pertai... ...tion. 2 ...avi...

neurial landscape. For example, in two national surveys, about six to seven in 10 youth reported that they wanted to start a business of their own. The proportion expressing this desire was highest among Hispanic youth and African-American youth, ranging from 70 percent to 80 percent, respectively.[7]

Surprising and most encouraging was the degree to which the nation's youth wanted to learn more about entrepreneurship in school. More than 75 percent of the youth surveyed thought that it was *important* or *very important* for the nation's schools to teach more about entrepreneurship and starting a business.

A commitment to philanthropy also permeated the entrepreneurial thinking of youth. Nearly 70 percent of the young people in past studies expressed the opinion that successful entrepreneurs have an obligation to give something back to the community—in addition to the jobs they were creating or the taxes they paid.

Youth's attitudes toward the new winds filling the sails of our economy challenge many of the prevailing perceptions of the so-called Generation X. The national profile manifested in this younger generation is more aligned with what we call the E Generation: the entrepreneurial generation.[8]

A distinguishing feature of this new generation, besides their age, is that entrepreneurial attitudes are often joined with the idea that successful entrepreneurs have a responsibility to improve the community in which they live. Many youth express the view that it is not enough for a person to do well for him or herself; he or she should do well for society.

Predicting the Future

The above discussion may leave the impression that the future is a rosy one for the nation because of the entrepreneurial attitudes of young America. While there is indeed the potential for the future to be one of greater creativity, productivity and economic prosperity, there is much to overcome for that prospect to become a reality.

Survey results have already suggested the "poor quality of education" as a barrier to the entrepreneurial contributions that youth might make in the 21st century. Eighty-five percent of youth reported that they were taught "little or nothing" in school about entrepreneurship and business. Given this situation, it is not unexpected that many youth do not know much about entrepreneurship. In fact, when we administered a test probing basic entrepreneurship concepts to a national sample of youth, we found that they were able to supply correct answers to only 42 percent of the items. The low test scores were also highly correlated with low self-assessments: more than eight in 10 youth rated their knowledge and understanding of entrepreneurship as only fair to very poor.

A window of opportunity clearly exists for entrepreneurship education in America to achieve major impact. There is a significant shortfall with respect to the entrepreneurship knowledge and skills youth will need to start businesses or make entrepreneurial contributions to society. There is also a solid demand for more entrepreneurship education in the schools to meet the shortfall.

For Generation E to become fully functioning, however, significant changes will also be needed to address the subliminal bias against entrepreneurship in our youth's education. Today, curriculum and teaching practices are unabashedly oriented towards the mentality of "take a job," with little or no attention directed towards the potential for career growth and societal contributions in the entrepreneurial "make a job" mindset. The attitude toward work conveyed in the education of youth is that they are being prepared for a career in which they will be employed by some kind of small or large business entity. In this view of the world, the presumption is that the student will be taking a job someone else has already created.

This presumption, which permeates our school system, is in part a reflection of the historical belief that the large corporation was a preferred source of employment.[9] Unfortunately, access to learning about entrepreneurship or the entrepreneurial process is almost non-existent. Students are not afforded the opportunity to develop the knowledge, skills and mindset they will need to engage in entrepreneurial thinking—or to have the option of creating jobs by conceiving and starting new ventures.

Previewing Chapters to Come

These themes—interest in entrepreneurship, obstacles to entrepreneurship and education in entrepreneurship—are examined in more depth in the chapters that follow. The foundation for this study and the primary sources for the findings reported are three extensive surveys administered to national samples of three groups: youth, young adults (college students) and business leaders.[10] The surveys were prepared with the advice of national experts on entrepreneurship and with assistance from survey researchers at the Gallup Organization. The Gallup Organization collected the data through telephone interviews during 1998 and 1999.

In probing youth with respect to the key issues highlighted, the investigation has been focused on the 14 to 19-year-old age group. It is during this time in their lives that serious thinking is embarked upon concerning potential careers and the markets in which they would be most likely to seek employment. Certainly, many may have engaged in earlier explorations of these topics. However, this 14 to 19-year-old period typically spans the time when the first rounds of actions are actually taken that lead to concrete decisions related to career options. These decisions, in turn, and the perspectives from which they are made, have a dramatic impact on the available pool out of which our nation can hope to draw the entrepreneurs and entrepreneurial thinkers of tomorrow.[11]

Young adults were also surveyed for purposes of comparison with the viewpoints of youth. The young adults who were interviewed were 21-30 years old.[12] This age group was of interest because most of them were engaged in or had completed their college education (some with embedded workforce experience). The age of this group also matches up well with the beginning of the age span (24-40) in which most people start new businesses.

A substantial portion of this book also focuses on the specific content of curriculum for entrepreneurship. Additional surveys were developed to ascertain both youth and young adult views about the importance for high school and college graduates— and their degree of preparation in—skills that are valuable for starting a business or working for someone else. The Gallup Organization administered these instruments to national samples of youth[13] and to national samples of young adults (college students).[14]

The same surveys were given to business leaders who employ high school and college graduates.[15] The motivation for surveying business leaders was to secure their seasoned judgment about the level of preparation and the knowledge needed by high school and college graduates to be successful in starting a business or working for someone else. Their responses could then be compared with the views of youth and college students as a "reality check" on the latter two populations' perceptions.

Highlighting Chapter Themes

The next three chapters report key findings on entrepreneurship interest and entrepreneurship obstacles from the surveys of youth and young adults. The significance of the results also is analyzed with respect to the entrepreneurial generation (Generation E), their entrepreneurship readiness and the barriers to their aspirations.

Chapter 2 addresses in greater depth who comprises Generation E, and what their relationship is to the youth start-up phenomenon alluded to earlier. In addition to this generation's interest in entrepreneurship, factors are investigated which may influence their probability of moving from interest to action.

Chapter 3 delves into the mindset of the young population sampled and the degree to which that mindset is conducive to overcoming some of the intrinsic practical and psychological impediments to initiating entrepreneurial ventures.

In Chapter 4, youth and young adult perceptions are explored with regard to the external obstacles that might get in the way of their pursuit of entrepreneurship.

Chapter 5 consolidates the critical challenges driving the case for youth and young adult entrepreneurship education and identifies the core attributes which are the hallmark of entrepreneurship education. This chapter also highlights the varying educational emphasis appropriate to entrepreneurial initiators, to development and support teams, and to general stakeholders in the entrepreneurial economy.

Chapter 6 identifies and frames (in three layers of a pyramid) 28 specific types of knowledge and skill areas that are important to achieving success in the initiation, advancement and support of entrepreneurship and intrapreneurship—independent of context or organization.

In Chapter 7, national survey findings with respect to the knowledge and skill areas outlined in Chapter 6 are analyzed from the perspectives of youth, young adults and business. The views of all three groups are compared for two major contexts: for those who want to *start a business* and for those who will be *working for someone else.*[16]

Finally, Chapter 8 presents key conclusions derived from the findings and conceptual themes presented in the book. It also makes recommendations for facilitating and supporting the aspirations of our youth and young adults—the entrepreneurs and entrepreneurial thinkers of tomorrow—with emphasis on the profoundly significant role that can be played by education.

With this brief overview, we turn our attention in the next chapter to the fascinating entrepreneurial generation of youth and young adults that inspired this book.

Endnotes

1. See also Timmons (1999), Kourilsky (1998) or Petzinger (1999) for further discussion of this entrepreneurial revolution and its implications.

2. In fact, small businesses have been responsible for most of our recent job creation (SBA, 1999).

3. See Kourilsky (1998).

4. For further evidence to support these last two points, see Williams (1999).

5. Women's contribution to the entrepreneurial economy is important. Almost one in four businesses in the United States was owned by women in 1999. The number of women-owned businesses doubled in the past 12 years and now stands at more than

9 million. These businesses furnish jobs for 27.5 million workers and generate more than $3.6 trillion in sales annually (NFWBO, 1999).

6. These statistics are based on reports from the U.S. Department of Commerce (1998). Although these changes are impressive, their interpretation must be tempered by the realization that for the most part the *absolute* number and size of minority-owned firms are still relatively small and are inconsistent with minority demographic presence in the United States.

7. See Kourilsky and Walstad (1998), Walstad and Kourilsky (1998), and Walstad and Kourilsky (1999).

8. For the first use of this term, see Kourilsky (1995).

9. See Kirchhoff, 1994.

10. Not all the responses or questions that we used in the surveys are reported in the chapters that follow. We selected for the reader only the most important findings from the survey studies.

11. Survey sampling has associated with it a degree of sampling error that can affect the interpretation of results. At the 95 percent level of confidence, the maximum expected range of the sampling error for the n=1,148 youth sample surveyed was +/- 3.2 percentage points. This statement means that if 100 different samples of 1,148 youth were randomly chosen from the same overall youth population, then 95 times out of 100 the sample results obtained would vary not more than +/- 3.2 percentage points from the results that would be obtained if the entire population of youth were surveyed.

12. At the 95 percent level of confidence, the maximum expected range of the sampling error for the sample of 1,105 young adults was +/- 3.2 percentage points.

13. Two groups of youth were surveyed about their views of skills needed by high school graduates. Youth from lower socioeconomic backgrounds were surveyed in spring 1998. In spring 1999, youth from middle to upper socioeconomic backgrounds were surveyed. For the first group, the sampling error was +/-3.5 percentage points at the 95 percent level of confidence. It was +/- 3.1 percentage points for the second. The responses from both surveys were similar, so for the sake of parsimony in the

book, we combined the responses.

14. At the 95 percent level of confidence, the maximum expected range of the sampling error for the sample of 603 college students was +/- 4.0 percentage points.

15. Two groups of business leaders were surveyed about their views of high school graduates. The spring 1998 survey of business leaders asked questions about the knowledge and skill area needs and preparation of disadvantaged high school graduates. The spring 1999 survey asked business leaders the same questions about the knowledge and skill area needs and preparation of high school graduates from more advantaged backgrounds. For the first group, the sampling error was +/-3.7 percentage points at the 95 percent level of confidence. For the second group of youth, it was +/-3.5 percentage points. Because similar responses were found from both surveys, the combined responses were reported to avoid non-illuminating duplication.

    At the 95 percent level of confidence, the maximum margin of sampling error for the college-oriented group of business leaders was +/-4.0 percentage points.

16. See Kourilsky and Kourilsky (1999a) for survey data. This report also included data on parent and teacher perceptions of importance and preparation—as they related to disadvantaged/underserved youth.

Generation E, as in Entrepreneur

In recent decades the United States economy has shown significant growth in the number of start-up businesses and a complementary major expansion in the small business sector. In fact, this vital sector now produces more than half of the nation's private gross domestic product. Small businesses also employ more than five in 10 workers and account for more than six in 10 of the new jobs created in our economy. An even more striking bellwether may be the large number of people now engaged in entrepreneurial activity. In fact, about 13 percent of the non-farm work force are actually running a business on a full-time or part-time basis.[1]

Leading the Revolution

Unexpectedly significant in this entrepreneurial revolution has been the role assumed by those 30 years of age and under. A recent study of the 5.6 million persons going into business in 1996 found that three in 10 of all new business owners had yet to celebrate their 31st birthday. Moreover, among this 30-and-under group of venture initiators, about 40 percent were 26 years old or younger.[2] The entrepreneurship and entrepreneurial thinking of young people are making major contributions both to today's economy and to the economic future of this nation.

Furthermore, one sees reflected in many publications, news stories and even headlines an apparent acceleration of desire among our nation's youth to start a business. For those young people who want to initiate a venture, there are now an abundance of handbooks, many of which are themselves written by youth or young adults.[3] High school students, seeing market opportunities in computers, personal digital technology and the Internet, are using their technological skills to start new ventures ("Whiz Kids: Teens Becoming High Tech Entrepreneurs"). College undergraduates are exhibiting an entrepreneurial zeal not seen in past decades. In fact, students at some of the nation's best colleges and universities are starting businesses while attending school or are making plans to start one immediately after graduation ("In a Class by Themselves: Harvard Grads Saw Green Beyond the Ivy Bus"). Even those seeking an MBA degree are rethinking their decision, with some dropping out to start a business ("To B-School or Not to B-School").[4]

Expanding Entrepreneurial Interest

Youth and young adults' strong interest in entrepreneurship were evident in the survey studies underlying this book. When asked if they wanted to start a business of their own, the response of a 1999 national sample of youth, ages 14-19, was overwhelmingly positive. More than six in 10 said yes, as can be seen from the survey results reported in Table 2.1.

The large percentage saying "yes" to entrepreneurship is not a statistical fluke. It is in fact remarkably consistent with the responses of national samples of youth who were interviewed in two previous surveys in 1994 and 1995.[5] The conclusion suggested by all three surveys conducted is that youth preparing to enter the new millennium are strongly oriented toward grounding their initial careers in the practice of entrepreneurship.

The same entrepreneurship question was posed to a national sample of young adults, ages 21-30, drawing "yes" responses of similar percentage magnitudes. Slightly more youth than young adults said they were interested in starting a business, but that difference can be attributed to the fact that more young adults than youth had already started ventures at the time of the survey. When the two affirmative responses (*yes* or *already started*) are totaled, the percentages of those interested in entrepreneurship among youth and young adults are very close (61 percent versus 64 percent).

Exploring the Likelihood of Action

People may express interest in starting a business and still vary greatly in their perceptions of the probability that they would

TABLE 2.1: Want to Start Business of Own

Response	Youth (n=1,148)	Young Adults (1,105)
	%	%
Yes	61	58
No	37	35
Have already started one	0	6
Don't know	2	1

actually take action on that interest. The respondents were further probed in this regard with a question asking how likely they were to act on their interest. The response scale ranged from 5 to 1, where 5 represented *very likely* and 1 represented *not at all likely* to start a business.

As reported in Table 2.2, the survey revealed that more than four in 10 youth and more than five in 10 young adults gave their interest a 4-5 rating, indicating they were likely to very likely to start their own businesses. By contrast, fewer than two in 10 youth or young adults gave their interest a 1-2 rating that would suggest little likelihood of their pursuing the initiation of a business. From the perspective of this study's youth and young adult populations, the interest in entrepreneurship is not perceived as idle speculation, and a significant proportion believe it is quite likely that they will realize their dream.

Also of interest are the large percentages of youth and young adults selecting the middle position on the scale. Slightly more than four in 10 youth and three in 10 young adults chose the response midway between *very likely* and *not very likely*. What

TABLE 2.2: Likelihood of Starting Own Business

Response	Youth [†] (n=692)	Young Adults [†] (624)
	%	%
5 Very likely	14	24
4	29	27
3	43	33
2	12	11
1 Not at all likely	2	5
Don't know	0	0
[†] Only *yes* respondents to question about starting your own business.		

16

these results suggest are that many youth and young adults may want to start a business, but are not sure they will act on their aspirations. For this group to become true entrepreneurs, they probably will need to receive extra help. Such assistance may take many forms (e.g. personal encouragement from friends or family, mentoring by entrepreneurs or more education). This extra push could result in these potential but uncertain entrepreneurs moving into the "more likely" camp.

Spending Time on the Thinking Grid

Even among those youth and young adults who expressed an interest in starting a business, such interest could range from a passing whim to a product of considerable thought. Another potential indicator of a commitment to entrepreneurship is the number of years spent thinking about starting a business.

To investigate this issue, the "Yes" sub-sample of potential entre-preneurs (youth who wanted to start their own businesses) were asked how long they had been thinking about starting an enterprise. About five in 10 of the entrepreneurial youth surveyed had been thinking about starting a busi-ness for two years or more—a sub-stantial period of time. It is, of course, not surprising that young adults had thought longer about the possibility of starting a busi-ness than had youth. Seven in 10 reported they had been contem-plating starting a business for two years or more. The average for young adults was three and a half years versus two years for youth. These results reinforce

TABLE 2.3: Time Spent Thinking about Starting Own Business

Response	Youth [†] (n=692)	Young Adults [†] (624)
	%	%
1 year or less	49	29
2 years	25	26
3 years	8	10
4 years	5	6
5 years	3	11
6 years or more	5	16
Don't know	5	2

[†] Only *yes* respondents to question about starting your own business.

the likelihood indicators discussed in the previous section and are further evidence that most youth and young adults who want to start a business are serious about this objective. It is not a passing fancy.

Gauging Time Proximity

It is also important to know how long potential entrepreneurs believe it will be before they start their businesses. Those who say they are likely to start a business in less than five to 10 years are much more likely to achieve that goal than those who anticipate taking action many years in the future. Much can happen with the passage of time to derail even the most determined entrepreneur.

To gauge the time proximity for these potential entrepreneurs, we asked respondents how many years it would be before those who wanted to start a business thought they would act on their idea. The average response for youth was about eight years. Given that the youth we surveyed were 14 to 19 years old, this estimate means that most youth saw themselves starting a business sometime between ages 22 to 27—a forecast which aligns realistically with typical life patterns and historical data. This age period would be after college, for those who attend, and after the formative period of experience with the world of work for those who do not. It also falls within the beginning years of the most fertile period for people to become entrepreneurs: ages 24-40.

It is again not surprising that young adults' estimate of the time period before starting a business was much shorter than that of youth—five years, on the average. This forecast also aligned well with other data. The addition of the five-year estimate to the age range of the group surveyed suggests that young adults would start their new businesses between the ages of 26 and 35. As was the case for youth, this span falls well within the prime age period for people to become entrepreneurs.

Based on our surveys and review of evidence on business start-ups, there is clearly a deep pool of *aspiring* and *practicing* youth and young adult entrepreneurs in the United States. The spirit of enterprise this generation brings to business and community has

TABLE 2.4: Years Until Starting Own Business

Response	Youth [†] (n=692)	Young Adults [†] (624)
	%	%
1-2 years	7	28
3-4 years	11	14
5-6 years	27	27
7-8 years	14	2
9-10 years	27	12
11 or more years	12	5
Don't know	2	12

[†] Only *yes* respondents to question about starting your own business.

already transformed America, and will continue to do so well into the 21st century.

Equally important, they manifest an exceptionally strong belief in the importance of entrepreneurs "making a difference" in society by giving something back beyond the jobs they create and the taxes they pay. Many are committed to direct their entrepreneurial enthusiasm into channels that can improve their communities or help address pressing social issues. This combination of entrepreneurial spirit and "Peace Corps" mindset is the hallmark of the E Generation.[6]

Taking Advantage of Technology

Both positive and negative forces are encouraging the migration to entrepreneurship of a significant segment of young America. The pace and magnitude of technological change have been among the major constructive influences. Microprocessor applications and the Internet/World Wide Web alone have radically reduced traditional barriers to starting a business and have opened up opportunities in many new markets.

Another positive development has been a steady improvement since 1980 in the macroeconomic conditions that are vital for starting a business. A low and stable inflation rate has facilitated more accurate forecasting and made prices a more reliable indicator of market value. A general reduction in interest rates has reduced the cost of financial capital. Meanwhile, the flow of historic levels of funds into the stock market and venture capital firms has improved access to money for starting businesses (an effect especially apparent in the Internet "dot-com" sector).

In many respects the young have been in the best position to take advantage of these technological and macroeconomic trends. The E Generation has grown up using microcomputers and their software applications; scanners and personal digital assistants; telecommunications networks, the Internet and e-mail; and other types of new technology. They typically have had more direct schooling or experience in the high-tech arena than more mature workers. Often, the opportunities and the possibilities associated with new technologies are more apparent to them than to earlier generations. Finally, their enthusiasm and energy can overcome obstacles that would discourage someone less adjusted to the rapid pace of technological and economic change.

The success stories from our country's high-tech revolution have also captured the imagination of today's youth and young adults. The legends of Steve Jobs (Apple Computer, et al.), Bill Gates (Microsoft), Michael Dell (Dell Computer), Larry Ellison (Oracle), Scott McNealy (Sun Microsystems) and Jim Barksdale (Netscape), among others, were instrumental in establishing renewed respect for entrepreneurship among the young. Entrepreneurs are now seen as the business heroes of many young people from all types of backgrounds in much the same way that Thomas Edison, Henry Ford and John D. Rockefeller were viewed as business role models around the beginning of the 20th century. This remaking of the image of the entrepreneur also has been a contributory factor to the increased level of general interest in entrepreneurship and its educational components.[7]

Eroding Traditional Views

Negative forces have also been at work to rekindle interest in entrepreneurship among the young. Perhaps foremost among them is the erosion of traditional views of business careers, especially in the corporate world.

In the past, the standard assumption was that corporations would provide job security and benefits for employees. In return, employees would remain loyal to the corporation for much of their working lifetimes. The downsizing that began in the 1980s, however, and continued into the 1990s, destroyed this implicit understanding and loyalty. Job layoffs and restructuring created economic uncertainty and dislocations among workers, with the resulting insecurity affecting their children. In other words, workers became parents of a new generation who did not want to endure the job instabilities or indifferent treatment experienced by their parents at the hands of the corporation.[8] In their language, this generation prefers to "make a job," rather than "take a job."

Other fissures in the corporate environment also encouraged young workers to fill the void by starting new businesses. Corporations outsourced jobs, used more part-time workers, and adopted just-in-time inventory management. Changes in employment and business practices such as these opened up new opportunities for self-employment and start-up businesses, and entrepreneurial thinkers were in the best position to take advantage. They tend to be more flexible in their approach to work and thus are willing to work outside the corporation or to accept part-time employment. They also are more willing to engage the risks (and corresponding potential rewards) implied by the changes in corporate policies.

Taking Control

To retain more control over their lives, a growing number of today's young people are adopting the "make-a-job" attitude. Through the self-employment of entrepreneurship, they are taking their careers into their own hands. They believe that when a person takes a job, he or she will always be subject to the vagaries of corporate life and the demands of the "boss."

In fact, in focus groups that included representation from ages 14 to 30, from both genders, and across ethnicities, two major points emerged. First, almost every member of the groups personally knew someone who had been "unexpectedly downsized." Second, they no longer believed in the corporate world's ability to provide any meaningful level of job security. On the other hand, a significant number of today's young people believe that people who make a job by becoming entrepreneurs have far more freedom and control over their work and their time, can better leverage their skills and abilities, and are more likely to be satisfied with the overall experience.

The survey data reported in Table 2.5 are consistent with these points as well as the results of related studies conducted by the authors. When youth and young adults were asked why they wanted to start a business, about four in 10 youth and five in 10

TABLE 2.5: Major Reason to Start a Business

Response	Youth [†] (n=692)	Young Adults [†] (624)
	%	%
To be my own boss	38	56
To earn lots of money	22	19
To use my skills and abilities	11	8
To overcome a challenge	11	6
To build something for the family	5	5
To help others	3	1
Other	7	4
Don't know	3	1

[†] Only *yes* respondents to question about starting your own business.

young adults said the major reason was *to be my own boss*. About another three in 10 youth and two in 10 young adults mentioned alternative major reasons which included *to use my skills and abilities, to overcome a challenge, to build something for the family* and *to help others*.

Clearly (and contrary to many stereotypes) "making lots of money" is not the major motivating reason for their becoming entrepreneurs. Only about two in 10 youth or young adults mentioned that factor as the key reason to start a business. The driving force for entrepreneurship among most of the young appears to have more to do with a need for personal freedom and fulfillment and less to do with pecuniary rewards. Moreover, as we have seen, much of the E Generation also hopes to achieve long-run philanthropic goals as a result of their entrepreneurial aspirations.

All of these trends bode well for entrepreneurship in the 21st century. Our youth and young adults are interested in actively pursuing entrepreneurship (and the entrepreneurial thought process)—and their interest appears to have "legs." They have thought about it for some time, "chasing the dollar" is not their primary goal, and they want to do it sooner rather than later. Some of these entrepreneurs are already at work changing the face of America. Others are in what might be thought of as an "incubation phase," seeking avenues to become better prepared for entrepreneurship once the time is right to take the plunge.

The next two chapters examine the various mindsets of youth and young adults and how conducive they are to the achievement of their entrepreneurial objectives. The chapters also explore their perceptions of external barriers to the pursuit of entrepreneurship. It is important to keep in mind that, although many may never become entrepreneurs *per se*, they all have the potential to bring the entrepreneurial spirit and its creative thought processes to their chosen work in business, education, government, philanthropy or any other sector of the economy.

Endnotes

1. Small Business Administration (1997).

2. National Federation of Independent Business (1996).

3. One recent example, *Better Than a Lemonade Stand: Small Business Ideas for Kids*, was written by a teenager (Daryl Bernstein) to provide entrepreneurial ideas targeted for fellow teenagers. Another entry in this burgeoning market is *Young Entrepreneur's Edge: Using Your Ambition, Independence and Youth to Launch a Successful Business*. It offers practical tips on starting a business for twenty-something job-seekers and was penned by a 26-year-old entrepreneur, Jennifer Kushell.

4. For the "Whiz Kids: ..." story, see *USA Today* (April 30, 1999, pp. 1-2B). See also "Ambitious Teens Take Ideas to the Bank," *USA Today* (June 21, 1999, p. 3B). For the college "Harvard Grads ..." story, see *Business Week* (March 29, 1999, p. ENT24). See also "Stanford State of Mind: Entrepreneur-included Biz Grads to Take on Tech World," *USA Today* (June 14, 1999, p. 1B). For the MBA story, see *Business Week* (March 18, 1996, pp. ENT24-25). See also "This Generation is All Business: Young Entrepreneurs Ride Waves of Technology, Cheap Capital, and Boundless Optimism," *Business Week* (March 1, 1999, pp. ENT4-8).

5. For further discussion of this point, see Chapter 2 in Walstad and Kourilsky (1999).

6. See Kourilsky (1995) for additional discussion.

7. For a discussion of pre-college programs and curricula, see Kourilsky and Carlson (1997). For a discussion of university curriculum, see Young (1997).

8. See Tannenbaum, Jeffrey A, "Like Father, Not Like Son," *The Wall Street Journal*, Small Business Section, May 24, 1999, p. R24. Also see Williams, Geoff, "2001: An Entrepreneurial Odyssey: Why the Next Century Will Belong to Entrepreneurs," *Entrepreneur*, April 1999, 106-113.

Attitudes on Entrepreneurship, Rites of Initiation

Our studies show that most young people want to start businesses of their own and have been thinking about new business ideas for a year or more. Respondents also say they are likely to start businesses while still young, which corresponds with the primary age range during which most entrepreneurs initiate ventures. These findings strongly reinforce the proposition that the current generation is indeed Generation E: the entrepreneurial generation.[1]

It can be a significant leap, however, to advance from being interested in starting a business to actually initiating an entrepreneurial venture. Moreover, the propensity of young people to take concrete action can be influenced by a number of mindsets. That's why it's helpful to examine the key "entre-initiating" attitudes of the young people who comprise the study samples.

The coined term "entre-initiating" connotes attitudes conducive to (although not necessarily sufficient for) overcoming some of the natural psychological and practical impediments to the development and start-up of new businesses. Compared in the following pages are survey results on entre-initiating attitudes among youth and young adults who were, and were not, interested in starting a business.

Measuring Multiple Attitudes

The Entre-Initiating Attitude Profile was developed by entrepreneurship expert Ed Moldt and the authors of this book. It consists of multiple-choice decision-scenario questions covering three topics: income risk and deferral, money usage and investment, and business initiation. The length of the instrument (10 items) and the topic areas selected were optimized to probe a key selection of entre-initiating attitudes while accommodating the practical length constraints of telephone call survey instruments for large national samples.

How valid and reliable were the measurements of the Entre-Initiating Attitude Profile? To find out, the initial design of the items was carefully cross-checked against current research literature on entrepreneurship ventures and the founders who start them.

The Profile's items were written to be interpreted easily by youth or by young adults. Each decision-scenario item presented multiple decision options, one of which was substantially more "entre-initiating" than the others. Item response choices were independently evaluated by expert entrepreneurs, as well as by entrepreneurship educators, to determine further which ones would reflect the most entre-initiating attitudes. Survey experts at the Gallup Organization were also asked to review and adjust question wording to minimize potential bias and eliminate possibly misleading terms.

Field test results with entrepreneurs, non-entrepreneurs and youth participating in an entrepreneurship education and readiness program confirmed the initiation-enabling role of the attitudes measured by the Profile. Further, the field test results for the high school and college students in the program showed that, as measured by the Entre-Initiating Attitude Profile, their entre-initiating attitudes increased significantly between the beginning and the end of the program.

Viewing Score Variations

Possible scores on the Attitude Profile range from a low of zero to a high of 10, but are not intended to be interpreted as measures of entrepreneurship IQ or knowledge. Nor should they be viewed as an absolute attitude litmus test for entrepreneurship initiation. The Profile is more analogous to a screening test. It can provide a rough indicator for the respondent's **current** attitudinal readiness to "seize the moment" and initiate an entrepreneurial venture.

It is important to keep in mind that such attitudinal readiness can also vary dramatically with both time of life and circumstances of life. For example, there are a number of young adults who might find their attitudinal readiness increasing noticeably once their education (and loan obligations) was largely behind them.

You may also know of people from differing segments of the economy who, in all likelihood, would have scored quite low on the Attitude Profile during the mainline employment years leading up to their retirement—but whose attitudinal readiness increased dramatically after they discovered they were not suited to their post-retirement lifestyles, and instead embarked on a variety of venture start-ups.

In other words, people's entre-initiating attitude readiness can be very much a function of their **current perceptions of the opportunity cost of starting a business**. Changes in circumstances and the passage of time often modifiy these perceptions. In particular, life changes which reduce a person's perceived opportunity cost of starting a venture (e.g. fewer personal obligations to chafe from lack of sufficient attention, fewer career opportunities to be foregone, or less schooling to be deferred) might be very likely to increase that person's entre-initiating attitude readiness.

On the other hand, as valid measures of respondents' current entre-initiating attitudes, one **would** expect the average scores of entrepreneurs on the Entre-Initiating Attitude Profile to be significantly higher than the average scores for non-entrepreneurs. That is, in fact, what was observed during field-testing of the instrument.

The survey results reported in this book were similarly predictable. Even though not all young people interested in starting a business take action on their vision, one would expect their entre-initiating to produce average scores significantly higher than those who expressed **no** interest in starting a business.

The sections that follow first discuss overall survey results in terms of what they reveal about differences in entre-initiating attitudes among young people. The discussion then turns to individual items of the Profile, focusing on variations in entre-initiating attitudes relative to the three topic areas included on the instrument.

Reviewing the Big Picture

Comparisons of overall scores for both the youth and the young adult samples yielded results consistent with expectations. Youth who were interested in starting a business selected more attitude choices oriented toward entrepreneurship initiation than those not interested in starting a business (see Table 3.1). The variation in percentage is statistically significant and not likely to be the result of some chance factor.[2] Rather, it is indicative of a meaningful difference in the overall entre-initiating attitudes of youth in the two groups.

For young adults, the difference between the "Yes" (interested) and "No" (not interested) groups was even greater than for youth. Young adults interested in starting a business gave the most entre-initiating attitude response to 48 percent of the items. For comparison, those young adults who were not interested in

TABLE 3.1: Most Entre-Initiating Attitude Response to Profile Items

| | Interest in Starting a Business | | | |
| | Youth | | Young Adults | |
Responses	Yes (n=692)	No (422)	Yes (624)	No (398)
	%	%	%	%
1. Pay based on productivity	42	42	52	42
2. Pay by commission or fee	26	21	47	41
3. Paid more at end of 6 months	19	16	37	30
4. Go ahead and start the business	21	15	46	25
5. Purchase company stock	20	11	38	27
6. Invest in collectible items	10	6	13	9
7. Will lack financial resources	47	41	72	63
8. Accept offer if helped	76	58	84	64
9. Build leadership team	42	38	45	37
10. Listened more to customers	54	37	51	37
Mean %	36	28	48	38

starting a business gave the most entre-initiating attitude response to 38 percent of the items.[3] This larger overall difference for young adults may be related to the fact that for individuals nearer to the age when they anticipate they might actually start their businesses, a stronger cross-section of entre-initiating attitudes (i.e., a stronger stomach for uncertainty and ambiguity) is required to cross the threshold into the "interested" group.

Crossing the Threshold

Field testing results for the Attitude Profile also suggested an interesting entre-initiating attitude "threshold" value that appears to be correlated with the actual start-up of a new business. Almost all of the entrepreneurs field-tested scored at least a five or above on the Profile, whereas almost all of the non-entrepreneurs (not an entrepreneur and not interested in starting a business) scored below that level. The plausibility of this threshold is also supported by the fact that it represents a 50 percent entre-initiating response.

A comparison of this threshold with survey results shows that among those interested in starting a business, only 27 percent of youth and 56 percent of young adults met or exceeded it. Why do the entre-initiating attitudes of approximately one-quarter of youth and about one-half of young adults who are interested in starting a business fall short of this apparent attitude threshold for realizing their interest?

The answer may rest with three key considerations. First, most youth and young adults have received very limited, if any, education in entrepreneurship. Second, the problem is compounded by limited opportunities to meet or work with entrepreneurs and to be exposed to entre-initiating role models. Finally, career educational experiences are often oriented toward the idea of "taking a job" rather than "making a job."[4]

In short, the attitudes of youth and young adults have been shaped by an educational system that typically ignores, and often discourages, entre-initiating attitudes and entrepreneurial risk-taking.

In the following sections, each of the individual decision scenarios posed in the Attitude Profile are discussed. For each question, the reasoning underlying the identification of the most entre-initiating response is reviewed, and major findings derived from the response data collected are highlighted.

Making Decisions That Pay

Young people's views on earning an income and on income risk can be very telling components of their entre-initiating attitudes. The proclivity to accept manageable income risk in exchange for higher potential income reward is one of the core attitudes of the initiator, because entrepreneurs must be willing to invest resources in and start ventures which—even if well-planned and thought through—carry no guarantee of success.[5]

Another key attitude conducive to entrepreneurship initiation is the preference to have income linked both to quality of effort, and to the degree to which that effort produces successful results. Closely related to this attitude is the desire for personally achieving successful results and for such personal accomplishments being tangibly recognized.[6] For individuals with such preferences, pay schemes that reward individual effort and achievement are characteristically more desirable than fixed rates of pay based primarily on time spent on the job.

The first survey question asked about the preferred method for earning an income. Respondents were given the choice of earning an income with a set rate of pay per hour or per month, or of having their rate of pay depend on productivity. Based on the preceding discussion, it is not surprising that the productivity response is viewed as more indicative of an entre-initiating attitude.

About four in 10 youth and five in 10 young adults preferred to be paid based on their productivity. Among youth, there was no significant difference on this question between those who were interested in starting a business and those who were not, perhaps because they had less experience in the job market. There was, however, a significant difference of about 10 percentage points in the expected direction for young adults. Those young adults who desired to start a business were more likely to want to be paid based on productivity.

In the second question, the pay issue was explored in a slightly different manner. Here, the focus was on the method of pay that would be perceived to be most likely to generate a high potential income. Being paid a commission or fee per item sold is the most entre-initiating response because it translates to expectations of greater rewards when working under a pay-for-performance scheme that (again) hinges on personal productivity.

For this question, respondents were provided three viable

TABLE 3.2: Income Items

| | Interest in Starting a Business | | | |
| | Youth | | Young Adults | |
Responses	Yes (n=692)	No (422)	Yes (624)	No (398)
	%	%	%	%
1. Which method would you MOST prefer to determine how much you earn?				
Same hourly or monthly rate of pay	53	52	43	51
Rate of pay based on productivity [†]	42	42	52	42
No preference	4	5	4	6
Don't know / Other	1	2	1	1
2. Which method of pay do you think is MOST likely to provide a higher potential income? A person who is paid:				
An annual salary	40	39	29	31
A regular weekly wage	33	37	23	27
A commission or fee per item sold [†]	26	21	47	41
Don't know / Other	1	3	2	1

[†] most entre-initiating attitude response

choices, instead of two. Because youth typically have little exposure to the concept of commissions, the percentage of entre-initiating responses selected by youth for this question might be expected to be lower than that for the first question. This expectation was borne out by the data. Only about a quarter of youth who were interested in starting a business preferred the higher income potential of being paid a commission or fee per item sold, in contrast to almost half of young adults who expressed that preference.

The survey results for this question also reflected a significant difference between the entre-initiating attitudes of those who were interested in starting a business and those who were not.

The differences in responses to the commission and fee option were evident for both youth and young adult samples.

A third income question concerned preferences with respect to timing of income, traded off against amount of income. (Most entrepreneurs are willing to defer receipt of income if they believe the delay will ultimately result in higher real income or return on their investment.)

For entrepreneurs who start new businesses and employees who work in them, stock options are a popular method for implementing such deferred payments. They work on the principle that if people are willing to invest effort in an enterprise while being patient and accepting some risk, there is the potential to be rewarded with future high stock market valuations. However, because most of the survey population could not be relied upon to be familiar with stock options or how they actually work, time-preference questions were formulated as follows: If they were to work part-time for a new business, would respondents prefer to be paid sooner at a lower hourly rate—or much later, but at a higher hourly rate?

Most young people appeared to have a short time horizon when it came to being paid, and did not exhibit entre-initiating attitudes in their decision-making on this question. More than eight in 10 youth and more than six in 10 young adults preferred to be paid less sooner (within a week or in two months) rather than more later (in six months). Only among young adults who wanted to start a business was there a significantly higher preference for a delayed, but higher, hourly wage when compared with those who did not want to start a business.

It is a fact that when an entrepreneur starts a business there is no assurance of when, or if, it will be successful. New ventures can take years to turn a profit. Entrepreneurs are sustained by their willingness to accept risk and lower income over the short-term to

Table 3.2: Income Items (continued)

| Responses | Interest in Starting a Business | | | |
| | Youth | | Young Adults | |
	Yes (n=692)	No (422)	Yes (624)	No (398)
	%	%	%	%
3. If you were offered a part-time job for two months at a new business, how would you want to be paid?				
$8 / hour; paid at end of week	51	47	34	37
$12 / hour; paid at end of two months	30	37	27	30
$16 / hour; paid at end of six months [†]	19	16	37	30
Don't know / Other	0	1	2	3
4. Bill developed a plan for a new business he wants to start. However, in the next three years, he expects to earn much less at this new business than he would if he took a job at another company. What would you do in Bill's situation?				
Get more business education and experience	69	66	42	48
Go ahead and start the business [†]	21	15	46	25
Forget business plan and take other job	10	18	11	26
Don't know / Other	0	1	2	2
[†] most entre-initiating attitude response				

develop an enterprise, believing that they have the potential to garner a higher income later as the business becomes profitable.[7]

Entrepreneurs also believe in following their business dreams. They are committed to building a better product, or offering a better service they have conceived. Worrying about immediate payment for work is not foremost in the minds of the initiator. It is the pursuit of the goal that drives the entrepreneur.[8]

To probe entre-initiating attitudes toward acceptance of risk in the pursuit of a business vision, the fourth question presented youth and young adults with several options for a hypothetical person who was sufficiently interested in an entrepreneurial concept to have already developed a business plan for it. One alternative involved starting up a venture to pursue the business concept. However, that alternative also included the expectation that income in the first three years would be less than that assured by another alternative, which was to take a job at another company offering higher income for the first three years.

Although only about two in 10 youth who wanted to start a business opted for the most entre-initiating response—*go ahead and start the business*—that fraction was still about one-third larger than that for youth who were not interested in starting a business. Of the young adults who themselves were interested in starting a business, a substantially higher percentage (about four in 10) manifested preference for this response. That percentage was nearly double the percentage of young adults in the "not interested" group who favored the same response.

Working with a Windfall

The uses to which people put money can also provide illuminating insights about their entre-initiating attitudes. If you were given a gift of a substantial amount of money, say $20,000, what would you do with it? Would you spend it on a major consumer product? Would you use it to purchase tickets to a major sporting event for yourself and your friends? Would you put it into a savings account? Would you invest it in stocks or bonds? These choices were offered to youth and young adults in a fifth question.

Entrepreneurship initiation is facilitated by an orientation towards long-term wealth-building and a tendency to limit the use of money on discretionary purchases, so that it may be conserved for investment opportunities.[9] A mindset that tends to favor higher "educated" risk investments with their greater reward potential over extremely "safe" investments with their lower reward payloads is also conducive to embarking on new ventures.[10]

The possible responses to the fifth question included two immediate consumption responses, either of which would use up all of the $20,000 gift money immediately. There were also two investment options: putting the money in a savings account and

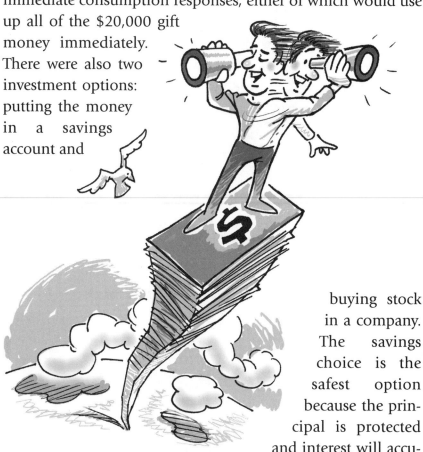

buying stock in a company. The savings choice is the safest option because the principal is protected and interest will accumulate, but it is likely to generate a lower return. There is more risk involved in purchasing the stock of a company, but the potential return is greater because the stock price can appreciate in addition to any dividends that may be paid.

The most entre-initiating response would be to *invest the funds in a company stock*. It reflects a willingness to defer the immediate gratification of "consumption" purchases and to accept a higher level of investment risk in exchange for potentially higher investment returns.

The majority of youth, however, would put the money into the safer investment option: the savings account. Fewer than one-fourth of our youth respondents selected the higher risk/higher (potential) return option of purchasing shares of a company stock. Nevertheless, among those youth who were interested in starting a business, the fraction who did select the most entre-initiating response was nearly double that recorded for youth not interested in starting a business.

TABLE 3.3: Uses of Money

	Interest in Starting a Business			
	Youth		Young Adults	
Responses	Yes (n=692)	No (422)	Yes (624)	No (398)
	%	%	%	%
5. If you received a $20,000 gift, which use of that money would you MOST likely choose?				
Put money in a savings account	54	63	41	54
Purchase a major consumer product	22	23	13	13
Purchase shares in a company stock [†]	20	11	38	27
Purchase tickets for self and friends to a major sporting event	3	3	1	0
Don't know / Other	1	1	6	6
6. If you were offered investment opportunities for half the savings you have accumulated, which choice would you MOST prefer?				
A savings account	60	64	51	57
Invest in collectible items or products [†]	10	6	13	9
No preference	29	29	35	32
Don't know / Other	1	1	2	1

† most entre-initiating attitude response

Overall, our results suggested less risk-averse preferences for young adults. Although almost half of young adults also would put the gift money into a savings account, more than a third still displayed the entre-initiating attitude to make the stock investment. In addition, the percentage selecting the stock investment option was substantially higher among those who wanted to start a business than those who did not.

The sixth question was similar to the fifth, but proved to be the "toughest" for both youth and young adults in terms of selecting the most entre-initiating response. Respondents were given the choice of putting half of their savings in collectible items or leaving the money in the savings account. The savings account option drew the most response—about six in 10 youth and five in 10 young adults.

The more entre-initiating choice would be to take the money and invest it in collectible items. Such items, when carefully researched and chosen, often have great potential to appreciate in value. Again, there is higher risk with this choice, but also the potential for higher return. Collecting things is a common avenue that has led people to become entrepreneurs by evolving a hobby into business.

Only about one in 10 youth or young adults selected the more entre-initiating choice. Lack of familiarity with the general term "collectible" as an investment concept may have played a role in the low selection results. Survey interviewers, when queried by puzzled respondents, were careful to explain the question in terms likely to be familiar to their age context (e.g. Pokémon cards, stamps, Beanie Babies, etc.). It is also possible that a number of respondents may have been too embarrassed to ask for clarification.[11]

Looking at Limitations

As discussed earlier, entrepreneurs believe intensely in what they are trying to accomplish and its potential for success. This belief is also linked to an entre-initiating mindset that is not hindered by fear of failure that might dilute an individual's determination to start a business.[12]

Neither are typical entrepreneurs perfectionists. They accept that their skills and experience may be limited in some respects, and that they might benefit from more education. However, people with attitudes conducive to entrepreneurship initiation believe they will be able to work around such constraints. They do not allow those limitations to hinder the decision to move forward with their business concepts.

Peer pressure and opinions have little influence on those with entre-initiating attitudes. Committed to their goal, they do not let the views of others dissuade them from their objective to start a business venture.

One genuine non-attitudinal concern for entrepreneurs is finding the resources to start their businesses. Even those with entre-initiating attitudes have legitimate cause for concern about marshaling the required funding for a venture start-up.[13] Financing is a necessary component of the fuel that enables the entrepreneurial engine to run.

The seventh question probed potential reasons people might give for not pursuing their business ideas to the point of venture start-up. The issues discussed above were reflected in the possible responses to question seven and in the identification of the most entre-initiating response: *concern about lack of financial resources*. The largest percentages of both youth and young adults selected this response. There were also significant differences in the percentages selecting this response among those who were interested in starting a business, and those who were not interested. The differences skewed in the expected directions for both youth and young adults.

Also of interest about the results from this question is the large

TABLE 3.4: Views of Starting a Business

| | Interest in Starting a Business | | | |
| | Youth | | Young Adults | |
Responses	Yes (n=692)	No (422)	Yes (624)	No (398)
	%	%	%	%
7. Suppose you came up with a good business idea after finishing your education. Which reason would MOST likely keep you from turning that idea into a new business?				
Concern that you will lack financial resources [†]	47	41	72	63
Concern that you might fail	28	30	15	20
Concern that your skills are not adequate to start the business	18	21	9	13
Concern with what your peers might think	4	7	1	2
Don't know / Other	2	2	3	2
8. A family friend is retiring from her business in which you are an employee and offers to turn it over to you to own. Which answer would you MOST likely give her?				
Would accept if she is available to help [†]	76	58	84	64
Would be afraid to try because your have never done anything like this	9	16	5	9
Cannot accept because you don't know what to do	9	12	4	6
Not interested	6	14	5	21
Don't know / Other	1	1	2	1

[†] most entre-initiating attitude response

percentage of youth who chose the non-entre-initiating responses. Regardless of their being interested or not interested in starting a business, almost three in 10 youth identify fear of failure as the most likely inhibitor to their becoming entrepreneurs. Another two in 10 are worried about the adequacy of their skills. Although these immediate concerns of youth run counter to more entre-initiating attitudes, it is important to remember that the concerns are not necessarily part of their permanent mindset. These youth may simply be evolving, and not yet at the entre-initiating "readiness" stage. At some later point, they may well reach a stage when they are more comfortable in general with an entre-initiating perspective, and in particular with the personal and financial trade-offs the aspiring initiator must make.

The eighth question posed the following hypothetical situation. Assume that you had a family friend who was retiring from her business in which you were an employee. She offers to turn over the business for you to own. Would you be willing to accept the offer if she were available to help you?

The entre-initiating response in this case would be to accept her offer—and that is the response selected by about seven in 10 youth and young adults. In this case, where a great opportunity is presented to young people to step into an existing entrepreneur's shoes, they would take it.

Especially striking about the results for this question are the sizable variations in the responses of the "Yes" (interested in starting a business) and "No" (not interested in starting a business) groups in each sample. The percentage selecting the "would accept" response was about 20 points higher for the "Yes" group than for the "No" group, for both youth and young adults. Perhaps due to the immediacy, clarity of the opportunity, and tangible nature of the commitment required to accept the offer, this question appeared to elicit some of the sharpest contrasts in entre-initiating attitudes between those interested and not interested in initiating a venture.

Growing a new business into a successful one is difficult. One key element of such success is building a strong leadership team for the business.[14] As a start-up venture expands in size and scope, that team is increasingly relied upon to shape the character of the enterprise and manage its growth. Finding the right individuals with whom to share leadership of the business and getting them to work as an effective and cohesive group over time are some of the most complex obstacles facing the entrepreneur.

Question nine was designed to elicit the perceptions of youth and young adults with respect to the relative difficulty of long-run business start-up challenges. The most entre-initiating response was *building an effective leadership team*. The other response options all deal with issues that, although potentially thorny in their own right, do not enjoy a comparable track record of difficulty **over time** across all forms of business initiation. Imagination, intelligence and research will usually bring to heel the problem of finding a good idea for a business. Locating a suitable building to house the business is a practical problem that typically can be solved with the help of knowledgeable consultants. Similarly, identifying a competent accountant or lawyer for the business is for the most part a matter of gathering information and referrals—and doing some screening.

About four in 10 youth and young adults manifested the entre-initiating attitude that *building an effective leadership team* was the most difficult challenge to surmount over time among the choices given. In addition, those youth and young adults who desired to start a business were more likely to exhibit this attitude than those who did not.

Interestingly, the results also show that for both youth and young adults, the "No" (not interested in starting a business) group was significantly more likely than the "Yes" (interested) group to have the attitude that finding a good idea was the obstacle most difficult to overcome over time.

A final question posed another hypothetical situation, this one exploring attitudes about why a new business might have

45

failed. The most entre-initiating attitude recognizes that in a market economy, consumer sovereignty is a key reality—especially for start-up ventures. In the event of a business failure, the initiator mindset does not blame the customer for the business' demise, nor does it challenge the personal appropriateness of the impulse to start a business. The initiator realizes that for

Table 3.4: Views of Starting a Business (continued)

	Interest in Starting a Business			
	Youth		Young Adults	
Responses	**Yes** (n=692)	**No** (422)	**Yes** (624)	**No** (398)
	%	%	%	%
9. If you were interested in starting a business, which do you think would be MOST difficult to achieve over time?				
Building an effective leadership team †	42	38	45	37
Finding a good idea	29	36	27	37
Locating a suitable building	14	15	13	12
Identifying a competent accountant or lawyer	14	9	13	12
Don't know / Other	0	2	2	2
10. Assume that you created a new business and ran it for a few months. You then closed the business because sales were lower than expected. Which statement would BEST describe how you think you would feel about closing the business?				
You should have listened to your customers more †	54	37	51	37
You learned that running your own business was not for you	33	54	24	50
You think people made a mistake in not buying your business product	11	8	17	9
Don't know / Other	2	1	8	4

† most entre-initiating attitude response

new businesses to succeed, entrepreneurs need to listen very closely to their customers. Failure to do so typically dooms nascent enterprises.

Almost half of youth and young adults selected the most entre-initiating response: *you should have listened to your customers more*. Additionally, for both youth and young adults, this question produced dramatic differences between the percentages who selected this response among the "Yes" (interested) and the "No" (not interested) groups.

Concluding Thoughts

Clearly, many youth and young adults are interested in starting a business. However, such interest must be blended with entre-initiating attitudes to achieve the chemistry needed to embark on the initiation of entrepreneurial ventures.

The Profile discussed in this section was introduced as a first-round screening instrument for such entre-initiating attitudes. The data gathered through this instrument revealed that youth and young adults who were interested in starting a business had significantly more entre-initiating attitudes than youth and young adults who were not interested. However, there was still substantial room for enhancement of those attitudes to the levels manifested by successful entrepreneurs.

On the other hand, respondents scoring high on the Profile are not necessarily going to become "initiating" entrepreneurs. High scores simply suggest that, at the current time, respondents appear to manifest more of the attitudes that signal having the "stomach" for the uncertainties, ambiguities, trade-offs and long-term issues of actually starting a business. Similarly, respondents scoring low on the Profile are by no means precluded from becoming entrepreneurs. Their "stomach" for starting a business—or entre-initiating attitude readiness—may well increase as the circumstances of their lives reduce the perceived opportunity cost of embarking on the initiation of business ventures.

If they are to realize their goals of starting businesses, youth and young adults need to be more entre-initiating in their attitudes and entrepreneurial in their thinking. In addition to such "internal" adjustments, however, several external obstacles must be overcome—an issue addressed in the next chapter.

Endnotes

1. See Kourilsky (1995).

2. It should also be remembered that the differences in percentages are limited by the number of items on the attitude survey. If we had included more items of a similar nature on the attitude survey, it is quite likely that the differences in percentages would have been much greater.

3. For this analysis, we omitted those young adults who reported they had already started a business (6 percent of the entire young adult sample). We would expect that the entre-initiating attitudes of this group would be higher than even those young adults who were interested in starting a business. In fact, we did find significant score differences between these two groups. Young adults who had already started a business gave the most entre-initiating response to 56 percent of the questions compared with 48 percent for young adults who said they were interested in starting a business. We could not do a similar analysis with youth because there were too few individuals in our sample who reported that they had started a business.

4. See Kourilsky (1995).

5. This point needs some qualification. Entrepreneurs tend to take calculated risks of a moderate nature about which they have "done their homework." They generally are not "random" or foolish risk-takers, and will tend to avoid unmanageable risks and risks that are not proportionate to potential rewards. For a further discussion of the research literature on risk-taking and risk-avoidance by entrepreneurs, see Stewart (1996) or Miner (1997).

6. The need for achievement has long been studied among entrepreneurs. For a review of this literature and an interesting empirical study, see Stewart (1996) and Morris (1998).

7. See Voth and Myer (1993).

8. For examples to illustrate this point, see O'Reilly (1999).

9. See Stanley and Danko (1996).

10. See Stanley and Danko (1996).

11. For these age groups, the sixth question manifested the least discriminating power—perhaps because it was difficult for the respondents to make the leap from collectibles to entrepreneurial activity. This question may be dropped or replaced in future versions of the Attitude Profile.

12. See O'Reilly (1999) for a discussion of this point and the next two that follow.

13. Brophy (1997) discusses financing issues and research.

14. See Smilor, R. W. and Sexton, D.L. (1996) or O. Isachsen (1996).

Obstacles to Entrepreneurship, Access to Education

Although many young people show strong interest in starting a business, numerous obstacles and barriers can get in the way of achieving that goal. While the previous chapter focused on internal hindrances related to entrepreneurial thinking and entre-initiating attitudes—the readiness to "seize the entrepreneurial moment"—this chapter deals with youth and young adult perceptions of external issues which may be preventing the realization of their dreams. Not surprisingly, entrepreneurship education (and the lack thereof) permeates this discussion, which begins with the sample groups' responses to a question specifically seeking their views of the greatest obstacles to starting one's own business.

Finding the Money

When we asked youth and young adults what they thought would be their greatest obstacle to starting their own business, one particular answer stood out. At the top of the list, drawing responses from five in 10 youth and six in 10 young adults, was "getting the financing." Difficulties in obtaining this resource is what our potential entrepreneurs think will most likely delay or stop them from becoming the entrepreneurial initiators of the future.

Certainly, obtaining financing is a major challenge for the budding entrepreneur. A person can have a good idea for a business and a well-developed business plan, but unless there is financing to start it, the business may never become a reality.

Finding financing, however, is a challenge that can be overcome. There are many sources of possible funds for starting an entrepreneurial venture. Some entrepreneurs "bootstrap" their venture with a small amount of start-up capital by using their own funds, borrowing on credit cards, and/or getting a loan from family members or friends. Others are able to obtain a loan from external sources such as a bank or another financial institution. Venture capital firms and private investor "angels" may also provide funding for fledgling businesses that meet their screening requirements.

These sources can be tapped if prospective entrepreneurs know how to find them and unlock people's willingness to invest. In reality, there are many sources of financing for an entrepreneurial venture—if it has merit, and if the entrepreneur has the persistence to pursue the search. Entrepreneurs who believe in their business ideas will find the funding to get their businesses started.

Appropriate education and training can do much to address the key issue of financing. Such an education can help people identify possible sources of funds (including strategies for minimizing the need for outside funding) and teach them how to tailor their business plans and approaches to obtain those funds. Education also reduces the psychological trepidation of aspiring entrepreneurs that often "freezes them in the headlights" and inhibits them from even trying to overcome the obstacle of start-up financing. Although education and training in entrepreneurship does not guarantee success in the pursuit of financing, it certainly betters the odds.

Overcoming Inertia

Getting started can be difficult with any big project, and starting a business is certainly no exception. Of all the many tasks to be accomplished, what should you work on first? Do you have the energy to take on the extra work and stress of creating a new business? Are you willing to accept the risk that the business might

TABLE 4.1: Greatest Obstacles to Starting Your Own Business

Response	Youth [†] (n=692)	Young Adults [†] (624)
	%	%
Financing	50	61
Getting started	22	18
More education	6	5
The good idea	4	4
Age or situation	3	5
Other	6	5
Don't know	8	4

[†] Only *yes* respondents to question about starting your own business.

fail? These and other questions often weigh on the minds of potential entrepreneurs and may keep them from taking actions to turn their dreams into reality.

This inertia obstacle, labeled as "getting started," was second in order of importance in both samples. It drew about two in 10 respondents from each group.

When youth or young adults cite factors related to getting started as a major obstacle, what they are really expressing is a mindset that makes the idea of starting a business look so imposing that the thought of doing it becomes overwhelming. Young people may know what they want to accomplish, but they do not know how to begin to get there. This lack of knowledge and inability to break a large task into doable pieces also inhibits action and makes them averse to taking the risk.

Education is one of the best options for overcoming the inertia obstacle. It breaks down what may appear as a monolithic and daunting task into its component parts so that each one becomes more understandable and manageable. More knowledge also lowers the perception of risk, because it helps people see what is possible and the steps one can take to achieve it. Entrepreneurship education—especially experience-based—is probably the most effective counter to the inertia problem.

Noting More Barriers

In response to the open-ended question about barriers, some youth and young adults did recognize obstacles related to their need for more education and training. Among the comments given were the need for more knowledge, concerns about managing or motivating people, and how to handle government regulatory requirements.

Also worth noting: a fourth obstacle category identified not being able to find a good idea or opportunity. Although often stereotyped as a major roadblock (if not **the** major roadblock) to

entrepreneurship, this obstacle was not thought of in that way by the young people interviewed. Indeed, only four percent of each sample mentioned it.

What these results suggest is that the large majority of youth or young adults interested in starting a venture did not perceive idea/opportunity generation as a particularly daunting task. For the small minority who may have difficulty in this respect, education in entrepreneurship could be useful for stimulating the thinking and creativity that underlies the generation of viable ideas and the concomitant recognition of market opportunities for those ideas. Even for the large majority who appear to be comfortable with their ability to dream up business ideas, classroom experience can be very helpful both for exploring whether their ideas really represent market opportunities and for refining raw concepts into focused ideas that are viable candidates for new businesses.

When the percentages for these four obstacles are combined, they account for more than eight in 10 of the responses. The remaining responses have to do with other obstacles such as "age or situation," about which little can be changed, or were obstacles cited by a very small number of youth or young adults.

Clearly, appropriate education can reduce the perceived magnitude of the barriers which dominated youth and young adult responses to the "obstacles to starting your own business" question. Such intervention can also help move them past the intent stage to the commitment and action stages for entrepreneurship initiation.

Rating Knowledge and Understanding

A general lack of confidence in the know-how required to initiate an enterprise was suggested by the first set of responses discussed in this chapter. This confidence level was probed more directly by explicitly asking youth and young adults to rate their knowledge and understanding of starting a business.

On a scale that ranged from excellent to very poor, how would most young people rate themselves? Would they consider themselves to be well prepared to start a business and give themselves an excellent or good rating? Or would they lack self-assurance and rate themselves as only fair, poor or very poor?

The answers to this question are important because they indicate whether young people think they have at least the cognitive competence to start a business. That sense of competence, which is based on knowledge and understanding, lays the foundation for the overall confidence that people need to start businesses. Interest and enthusiasm for starting a business is not enough. People also have to know and understand what they need to do to make the business a success.

Our findings show that a great majority of youth (76%) and young adults (69%) give themselves low ratings on their knowl-

TABLE 4.2: Knowledge and Understanding of Starting and Managing a Business

Response	Youth [†] (n=692)	Young Adults [†] (624)
	%	%
5 (Excellent)	5	6
4 (Good)	19	25
3 (Fair)	40	40
2 (Poor)	29	23
1 (Very poor)	7	6

[†] Only *yes* respondents to question about starting your own business.

edge and understanding of starting a business. Slightly more than a third of youth and about three in 10 young adults rated their knowledge and understanding of starting a business as *poor* or *very poor*. Another four in 10 in each group considered their knowledge and understanding to be only *fair*. These self-ratings indicate that those youth or young adults who wanted to start a business believe they lack the cognitive self-confidence they need to start a business, at least at this time in their lives.

By contrast, only about a quarter of youth and three in 10 young adults rated their entrepreneurial knowledge as either *good* or *excellent*. Among this self-assured group, however, the great majority (80%) gave themselves only a good rather than an excellent rating.[1]

Expected Source of Preparation

Youth also recognize the importance of education for starting a business. In an open-ended question, we asked them to discuss from what source they expected to derive (or had derived) most of their **preparation** for starting a business. The predominant response that significantly outweighed all others was "education in school," identified by nearly half the respondents.

TABLE 4.3: Source of Most Preparation for Business Venture

Response	Youth [†] (n=692)	Young Adults [†] (624)
	%	%
Education in school	48	24
Life experiences	9	20
Working at another business	7	23
Talking with other entrepreneurs	5	4
Talking with family	4	3
Learning from a family business	3	3
Reading about starting a business	1	3
Ability to spot an opportunity	1	1
Other	7	13
Don't know	14	7

[†] Only *yes* respondents to question about starting your own business.

For the other half of youth who wanted to start a business, the next five sources of preparation, in order of youth expectations, were "life experiences" (9%), "working at another business" (7%), and "talking with entrepreneurs" (5%), "talking with family" (4%), and "learning from a family business" (3%). These five sources can be interpreted as representing different forms of access to role models and, taken as a group, were identified by almost three in 10 youth.

Among young adults, education was also at the top of the source-of-preparation list—but the percentage citing it was only half of what it was for youth. Having moved into their mid- to late-20s, these young adults on the average have completed significantly more schooling than the youth sample. They can also be expected to have benefited from more experience in the workplace and from a broader variety of interactions with members of both the make-a-job sector and take-a-job sectors.

Given their experiences and perspectives, they appear to have developed higher preparation expectations for the access-to-role-model group of responses (selected by more than half) relative to the education-in-school response (selected by less than one-quarter).

Investigating High School Entrepreneurship Courses

The last two sections revealed high expectations for education as a source of preparation for starting a business in concert with the low self-ratings with respect to knowledge and understanding of how to start a business. These results suggest that young people, especially youth, believe that education is not meeting their preparation needs for entrepreneurship and entrepreneurial thinking. To probe this issue further, a simple measure of that education was investigated: the percentage of youth and young adults who had taken courses while attending high school (and

in a later section, college) in any area that might include some entrepreneurship or elements of the entrepreneurial process.

With respect to high school, the probe revealed that fewer than four in 10 of youth and young adults who were interested in starting a business reported

taking a high school course in either business or entrepreneurship. Of course, nothing is known about the content or quality of those courses taken. But regardless of their effectiveness, the percentage still suggests that more than six in 10 youth and young adults who are interested in starting a business receive no direct education in entrepreneurship or business in high school. Furthermore, the majority of courses available in business and entrepreneurship focus very little on the entrepreneurial process and typically are not targeted to the students bound for four-year colleges.[2]

There is a major cost to society when potential entrepreneurs fail to receive an effective education in entrepreneurship. The enthusiasm or interest they express in starting a business may not be transformed into action because they lack the knowledge needed to accomplish their goal. The nation loses because fewer new businesses get started, fewer new jobs get created and less entrepreneurial thought capacity is available to invest in the processes and enterprises that will lead to future economic growth.

It might be argued that the low percentage receiving entrepreneurship education in high school is appropriate because not all youth or young adults will start a business. However, such an edu-

TABLE 4.4: High School Business or Entrepreneurship Course

Response	Youth[†] (n=551)	Young Adults[†] (624)
	%	%
Business or entrepreneurship	38	36
Economics	47	58
Personal finance	30	40
[†] Only *yes* respondents to question about starting your own business.		

cation has benefits that go well beyond new business creation. As will be described in several of the next chapters, skills and knowledge gleaned through entrepreneurship education can enhance lives by making people more entrepreneurial in their thinking and in the ways they contribute in all areas of endeavor. This holds true regardless of their ultimate decisions about starting their own businesses or working for someone else in the private, public or not-for-profit sectors.

Evaluating High School Economics Courses

Course work in economics has a very complementary linkage to entrepreneurship education because it helps people understand how competitive markets work and how the macro economy functions. Entrepreneurs need to know about supply and demand. They need to know how prices and wages are determined in a market economy. They need to know how changes in monetary policy or the federal budget can affect the entire economy. In each case, changes in economic conditions and economic policy can directly or indirectly affect their ventures.

Less than half of youth reported taking an economics course in high school. Interestingly, a review of national transcript data suggests that only about 44 percent of high school graduates completed a separate course in economics in high school. This percentage is almost exactly the same as the estimate reported from the survey data, and certainly falls within the margin of sampling error.[3]

The estimate was higher for young adults, with almost six in 10 saying they had taken an economics course in high school. This larger percentage may well be a result of the higher likelihood of college-bound students having taken an economics course as part of "college track" preparation.

What the percentages suggest is that approximately half of youth do not take an economics course in high school. Of course, they can learn about particular micro- or macroeconomics concepts in other courses. But they never get a chance to pull all the economics content together and master the material through direct, formal instruction in a separate, integrated economics course. This situation contributes to a low level of economic literacy among youth that often continues into adulthood for those who either never go to college or never take an economics course in college.[4]

Assessing Personal Finance Courses

Courses in personal finance or consumer economics have the potential to contribute to skills needed by potential entrepreneurs. Instruction about household budgets, insurance purchases, investment options, career choices, tax alternatives and other personal decisions can be both essential and useful for anyone who wants to start a business. The economic decisions people must make for their personal households are similar in many ways to the business decisions they are called upon to make when starting and managing their own firms.

The survey results show that instruction in personal finance is also quite limited. Overall, only about three in 10 youth or young adults reported taking a personal finance or consumer economics course in high school.

Considering High School Curriculum

The piecemeal approach of today's high school curricula in areas related to the entrepreneurial process has contributed significantly to the poor quality and incompleteness of high school level entrepreneurship education. Subject areas such as economics, personal finance, business—and even entrepreneurship, in its rare appearances—are treated as discrete courses, with little tying them together.

For the more traditional major areas of the high school curriculum, such as mathematics, science, language arts and social studies, coherent sequences of courses have been developed that progress through well-defined sets of in-depth subject matter components. They are further integrated such that during their progression prior learning is systematically reinforced, complemented and expanded. In mathematics, for example, there are course sequences that cover basic algebra, geometry, advanced algebra and calculus. Equivalent progressions have been defined in the sciences that cover biology, chemistry and physics. There remains a significant need for the development of a similar sequence of integrated, in-depth courses covering business and personal finance, economics and entrepreneurship that all high school students would be encouraged to take.[5]

An analogous approach would also be of value for undergraduate liberal arts programs. One potentially effective solution is to structure a sequence of courses and field activities that allows students to earn an entrepreneurship certificate of emphasis as part of their baccalaureate degree.[6]

Graduating to College Courses

If high school students fail to receive an adequate education in entrepreneurship, can one rely on that education being back-

TABLE 4.5: College Business or Entrepreneurship Course

Response	Young Adults [†] (n=468)
	%
Small business or entrepreneurship	35
Other business courses, such as accounting, business law, finance, management, marketing	56
Economics	51
† Only *yes* respondents to question about starting your own business.	

filled for those who go on to college? Unfortunately, survey results do not suggest a positive response; the course-taking situation appears not to be any better at the undergraduate level.

One would hope it would be highly likely that those young adults who are interested in starting a business and who attended college would have taken a course in small business or entrepreneurship. The facts tell a different story. Only about a third of these young adults took a course either in small business or entrepreneurship.

The course-taking situation is better in two supporting areas for entrepreneurship or small business: other business courses and economics. Slightly more than half of the young adults did report they had taken other business courses, such as accounting, business law, finance, management or marketing. About half of this group also reported taking an economics course.

Overall, entrepreneurship education for most young adults

who want to start a business appears spotty and inconsistent at best. Given these results, it is not surprising that the self-ratings of knowledge and understanding of entrepreneurship among young adults were also quite low.

Learning about Jobs and Careers

There is one other issue that we see as a major problem in the area of entrepreneurship education at both the high school and college levels. Both the overt and "covert" focus of most job or career education that young people receive is on preparing to be hired and employed by someone else. Little attention is given to career education and training oriented toward entrepreneurial thinking and the option of creating a job by starting a business.

Consequently, most of the nation's young people are channeled into traditional career paths. The process does feed our country's supply of important employee functions, such as accountants, business managers, teachers, executive assistants, engineers and government officials. Unfortunately, this educational "tunnel vision" also leads them to think jobs are supplied by other people or organizations. They fail to learn that they too have the potential to create a job that may make the best use of their particular skills and insights.

Short-Changing At-Risk Youth

The channeling of our nation's young people into the employment marketplace is particularly damaging for at-risk youth. The relatively limited learning about entrepreneurship found today often occurs primarily in the home, through youth observation of or discussion with a family member who runs a business. Such ad hoc opportunities are, of course, more likely to be found in middle and upper class homes, providing the youth in those contexts with access to entrepreneurial role models and a chance to gain knowledge about what it takes to start and run a business.

65

In short, at-risk youth generally have far fewer opportunities within their families and their socioeconomic environment to learn much about entrepreneurship. The schooling they do receive typically focuses on job skill training and restricts their vision of the possibilities for productive employment. That vision tends to be a narrow one, bounded by minimum-wage jobs on one side and low-level management jobs on the other side.[7]

Lack of access to entrepreneurship education also has serious consequences for those youth from middle and upper socioeconomic backgrounds as they move into their young adult years. Many college students with more privileged backgrounds and successful academic records (including good grades, high SAT or ACT scores, and college degrees) become dissatisfied with the job market. They might think they are not paid enough for the work they do. They might be unfulfilled by the work they do for a company. They might feel insecure about their employment with corporations because of the threat of layoffs and the erosion of trust between employer and employee.

Looking for a better situation by job-hopping from one employer to another is a common expression of such dissatisfaction. Frequently, these youth "boomerang" back to their parents' homes as they attempt to sort out what to try next. Although many are interested in starting a business, nothing in their successful academic history prepared them for the entrepreneurial process of identifying and acting upon a market opportunity. They see no avenue to take their entrepreneurial interest and passion and combine it with their knowledge and experience to develop a market opportunity into a start-up business.

A large proportion of these displaced youths—if they are lucky—will probably secure an arbitrary job for which they may be significantly overqualified, for which they have no passion, and for which they are poorly paid relative to their education. They would like to have "made a job," but had no idea how to think like or become an entrepreneur. These young adults are also "at-risk" in the sense that they may well find themselves trapped in jobs and career paths for which they have no affinity—and without the entrepreneurial skills to create alternative options for themselves.

Through the creation of jobs and innovative products and services, the entrepreneurship of the "make-a-job" sector of our economy is accelerating the expansion of its signature role in the economic growth of our country. In parallel, the "take-a-job" sector is relying increasingly on the intrapreneurship of its workforce—the ability of associates to initiate, advance and support entrepreneurial thinking and behaviors that will help their ventures and institutions flourish in the new economic terrain. Youth, more than ever before, see the need for entrepreneurship and entrepreneurial thinking skills as key survival resources to help them navigate the increasingly challenging economic passages of the 21st century.

Their education in entrepreneurship will need to be a "real" one. Business management education that targets primarily the managers and executives of tomorrow will not suffice. What is needed is solid curriculum in entrepreneurship with the appropriate focus and ingredients to help youth and young adults become the initiating entrepreneurs and entrepreneurial thinkers of the future. The key attributes of such curriculum are the subject of the next chapter.

Endnotes

1. For survey data, see Kourilsky and Kourilsky (1999a, and forthcoming). In our previous book, results were reported from a short knowledge test on entrepreneurial topics that was given to a youth sample. A strong correlation was found between the low knowledge scores for many youth and their low self-assessment (see Walstad and Kourilsky, 1999, chapter 4).

2.   See Kourilsky and Carlson (1997).

3.   See Walstad and Rebeck (2000). Walstad (1994, pp. 109-136) presents data on course-taking patterns in economics or business in high schools over time.

4.   For a discussion of this issue, see Walstad (1998) and Walstad and Rebeck (1999). These articles are in two issues of the *Region* magazine of the Minneapolis Federal Reserve Bank that were devoted to the economic literacy problem.

5.   See Chapter 12 in Kent (1990) for more explanation of the entrepreneurship curriculum in high schools.

6.   Planning is under way for this approach to be modeled by the University of Iowa.

7.   See Kourilsky (1995) for more on these points.

Searching for Curriculum, Striving for Access[1]

How important is entrepreneurship education? Some major themes tell the story. First, youth and young adults have gone on record with respect to their strong interest in entrepreneurship and entrepreneurial thinking. At the same time, they have been direct about their shortfall of knowledge and skills for pursuing this interest—and their desire for schools to fill the gap. Moreover, their self-assessment coincides with the low level of entrepreneurship knowledge they demonstrate.

In short, they are in search of educational opportunities that will help them understand the role of entrepreneurship and acquire the knowledge and skills required for becoming successful entrepreneurs and entrepreneurial thinkers. Furthermore, students from all socio-economic contexts—at-risk, middle and upper—are being intellectually and economically disadvantaged by their lack of educational access to "make-a-job" thought processes, concepts and career options.

Another key theme revolves around the economic growth of our nation and its capacity for generating employment. Increasingly, entrepreneurship and entrepreneurial thinking are emerging as the dominant forces for the creation of new jobs, products and services. This is happening through the initiation and expansion of ventures, as well as through creative operating functions within ventures.

Much depends now (and more will depend in the future) on the ability of our educational system to help develop the intellectual and attitudinal platforms from which the entrepreneurs and entrepreneurial thinkers of tomorrow can launch their innovative efforts. Such platforms also will be important for increasing the (often intimidatingly) low likelihood of survival and long-run success for new ventures. Unfortunately, recognition of what content should lie at the core of entrepreneurship education has not kept pace with the compelling and accelerating case for it. This chapter explores what should lie at the core of "real" entrepreneurship education initiatives that can meet these challenges.

Identifying Three Attributes

The curricula of many schools and colleges focus on education for *business management* in well-intentioned attempts to tackle the less understood goal of *real entrepreneurship education.* One must begin, then, by examining what lies at the heart of entrepreneurship and contrast it with the different but complementary role of day-to-day functions involving business management.

True entrepreneurship is characterized by three critical attributes. The first is the identification or recognition of market opportunity and the generation of a business idea to meet the opportunity. The second is the marshaling and commitment of resources *in the face of risk* to pursue the opportunity. The third is the creation of an operating business organization to implement the business idea.[2]

Opportunity recognition is the cornerstone of the entrepreneurship process. This is the all-important crucible of creation, blending observation, market/customer insight, invention and

adaptation. What emerges are both the identification of an unful-filled desire of the marketplace, and the idea for a service or product to meet that desire at an acceptable price.

Having distilled an opportunity, the prospective entrepreneur must be willing and capable of securing the investment of resources to pursue that opportunity without any assurances of outcome or rewards. Acceptance of risk is an inherent aspect of starting a business. The entrepreneur must be both passionate and committed in pursuit of the opportunity, even in the face of this risk.

This commitment usually requires the entrepreneur to leverage both personal reputation and personal resources to advance the project. It also means he or she must be able to persuade others to make investments in the venture in the form of time, knowledge, energy, reputation and financial capital—all without any guarantee that the venture will succeed.

Finally, the entrepreneur must build from the secured resources a business organization that effectively delivers the product to its target customers. The entrepreneur and the business organization should never forget that it was these potential customers who, directly or indirectly, inspired initial recognition of the opportunity.

Examining Business Management

It is at this point in the entrepreneurial process—the creation of a business organization—that the key functions of business management take on greater importance for the development of the business. This stage of the process draws on such management functions as human resources, finance, marketing, selling and manufacturing to foster the growth of the venture.[3]

Although successful entrepreneurship does evolve into good business management during the implementation stage of a new venture, that is only part of the story. The seminal antecedents to business management are the three attributes of entrepreneurship—opportunity recognition, marshaling of resources in the presence of risk, and building a business enterprise.

Real entrepreneurship education can never succeed without focusing on these three attributes. Unfortunately, most of the instruction supplied in the name of entrepreneurship education focuses almost exclusively on the traditional management functions. Why? Probably because they are well understood and easier to teach.

How do the distinctions between entrepreneurship education and business management education fail to be realized in practice? Business projects from nominal programs in entrepreneurship are remarkably similar in the three ways they fall short.

First, the class is presented with a business idea, or votes as a group to pursue one from a list of ideas supplied by the teacher. This eliminates the opportunity recognition stage. Second, the class decides as a group how to allocate people to the management functions for the business, negating individual responsibility for the marshaling and commitment of resources. Third, the element of personal risk and reward is absent from the venture: money earned from the project is turned over to the class or school for redistribution to others, while losses are absorbed by the school or an outside sponsor.

A classic example of such an entrepreneurship project is having students assume responsibility for the day-to-day management of a school store. Another is the outside sponsorship of a micro-business formed by students for which they follow set guidelines, and in which there is no element of true risk.

Such programs, pursued in the name of entrepreneurship education, are usually well-received by students, teachers and parents. They are enjoyed as a welcome experiential departure from a didactic classroom dominated by teacher-talk and direction. They can also deliver some educational value through cooperative learning, a focus on management functions, and shared results.

These programs, however, miss the heart of the entrepreneurship process (and of entrepreneurial thinking). The students do not experience personally the search for market opportunity and the generation of a new business idea. They are not forced to accept the personal challenge of securing resources over which they have no control for a business idea that may not work. Nor do they take the risk of investing their own resources, time and even reputation in an entrepreneurship venture which may succeed or fail.

In short, the key personal experiences of entrepreneurship are either missing entirely, or are fatally compromised by group control of the project and intervention of the teacher and/or school administrators.

Inspiring the Initiators

Why are most of today's well-intentioned entrepreneurship education efforts missing the point? The problem stems from inadequate attention to the significantly different educational needs of three groups essential to the initiation, execution and support of entrepreneurship.

Entrepreneurship's implementation and support community can be segmented into three major constituencies: the initiator, the development and support team, and the stakeholders. The initiator has the ability and skills to identify opportunities with good market potential and the passion to pursue these opportunities in the presence of risk. The initiator sees what others have overlooked and is willing to take action where others may not.

In the initiator's hand, the intangible vapor of opportunity and idea is converted into tangible business realities of lasting value. He or she does so by meeting new market needs and creating new ways to meet existing ones. The initiator understands how to negotiate the chaotic and unpredictable process of organizing resources and talent to initiate a new business venture regardless of his or her level of control of the resources.

The initiator also has the commitment to put his or her own resources and reputation on the line in the face of unknown outcomes. Initiators are tenacious, rational risk-takers, comfortable with day-to-day ambiguity, and able to leverage divergent thinking into the creation of new business enterprises.

Only a select few seek this level of entrepreneurial activity. They are the highly committed, passionate strivers who have the attitudes and skills to start a business based on their determined vision of a great opportunity.

Recruiting Development/Support Teams

After shepherding both opportunity and business idea through the treacherous process of venture start-up and initial growth, the initiator will recruit a "development and support team" from the next layer if he or she wishes to move the venture into its next growth phase. In general, the members of the development/support team are not necessarily initiators themselves. However, they usually have a strong affinity for the initiator, a commitment to the integrity of the initiator's business vision, and a tendency to be entrepreneurial in their thinking and behavior.

The support team engages in innovative, pro-active and risk-taking applications of its group skills to scale up dramatically the venture's resources, processes and performance in key areas. These include human resources, finance, marketing, selling, development, manufacturing and general management. Such entrepreneurial contributions by the support team are critical to achieving significant growth after a venture hits its first major plateau in revenue generation.

A much larger population is attracted to the development and support team layer than to the initiator layer. However, the boundary between the initiator and development/supporter layer is reasonably porous in terms of both group characteristics and mobility. Initiators engage in entrepreneurial behavior as well as entrepreneurship. Members of development/support teams may ultimately become initiators by expanding their entrepreneurial actions and by engaging more directly in entrepreneurship.

Securing Stakeholders

Both the initiator and development/support team layers rest on a broader constituency of "stakeholders" in the continued growth of entrepreneurship and its positive effects on economic and personal developement. These stakeholders appreciate the qualities and accomplishments of the initiator and the development/support team. They also endorse policies conducive to entrepreneurship and entrepreneurial behavior. Although initiators and development/support teams are members of this layer, it also includes many more who subscribe to beliefs, commitments and values that may be referred to as entrepreneurism—but who currently are neither entrepreneurs nor actively involved in entrepreneurial ventures.[4]

This situation, however, can change. Again, it is quite possible for stakeholders to migrate to other layers, especially given their understanding of and commitment to entrepreneurship and entrepreneurial thinking. Individual life circumstances and education and training opportunities are some of the factors that might energize members of this constituency to move to the development/support team or initiator levels of entrepreneurship.

Ultimately, our country must be able to draw heavily on our youth population if the supply of future entrepreneurs is to keep pace with new opportunities inherent in existing and emerging technologies and our increasing needs for creative venture initiation and growth. Before moving to the final section of this chapter, it may be useful to apply the insights offered by Chapters 2 and 3 and attempt to answer the following: How many of our youth can we expect to enter the ranks of the entrepreneurship initiator?

Although there are no precise answers to this question, there are several plausible avenues for hypothesizing rough estimates. One possible approach might be to begin with the 61 percent of all youth who asserted that they wanted to start a business of their own (see Chapter 2). Among this subgroup, only 14 percent indicated that it was *very likely* that they would start a business. The intersection of the two response categories suggests that only about eight percent of all youth would be very likely to become initiators.

A similar approach would be to begin with the same 61 percent of youth who wanted to start their own business, and then focus on the 13 percent who scored at least one standard deviation above the "5" threshold on the Entre-Initiating Attitude Profile. Again, only about eight percent would appear to be destined to become initiators. For young college adults who are not already entrepreneurs, the percentage estimates for initiators (using the same approaches) range from 11 to 14 percent. Of course, there are many other ways to pursue such estimates, all of which would be controversial. Nevertheless, it is probably safe to speculate that no matter how the question is approached, these percentages—if not anemic—are certainly worthy targets for improvement.

Ensuring Education for All

Successful entrepreneurship and entrepreneurial thinking depends on the advocacy and efforts of all three constituencies: the initiators, the development and support teams, and the stakeholders. Real entrepreneurship education, integrated with appropriate economic education, can increase the membership and effectiveness of each of these constituencies.

Entrepreneurship-informed economic education improves both entrepreneurship and economic literacy. In turn, such literacy improvements help the stakeholder constituency understand free market functions and their interdependencies with the processes of entrepreneurship. They also provide more visibility for the variety of ways in which the stakeholder constituency benefits from the entrepreneurial economy.

77

The development and support constituency can also derive much benefit from entrepreneurship education initiatives that address the dimensions of entrepreneurial leadership.[5] These include providing vision and developing co-visionaries, focusing on opportunity and innovation, and ensuring that a top priority of the overall venture process is accountability to the venture's customers (and to the deliverables due those customers).

Also key are the concepts of self-generated motivation, a culture which embraces content and substance (in lieu of form and flash), and the fostering and rewarding of intelligent risk-taking. Members of the development and support constituency will be called upon to provide leadership and guidance for putting in place and maintaining cultures that emphasize these principles. In so doing, they maximize the probability of success for their organizations' or teams' ventures.

The most severe entrepreneurship education deficiency to

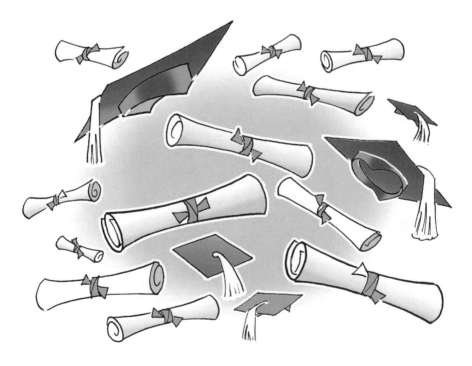

address involves the knowledge, skills and mindset needed to become an initiator. Some of today's economic education programs are already making contributions at the stakeholder level by promoting a broader understanding of how competitive markets function. Similarly, the business process skillsets and entrepreneurial behaviors of the development and support constituency are deriving some level of benefit from today's business management education efforts and from alternative instructional approaches such as cooperative learning and team building.

Unfortunately, entrepreneurship education for the initiator level is not even addressed by most of today's curricula—even those labeled as entrepreneurship programs. In the few instances where attention is given to the subject, the treatment is usually in terms of collections of desirable attributes such as tenacity and flexibility, sometimes combined with short discussions of the mechanics of business start-ups. Education and personal experience in core initiator areas such as opportunity recognition, marshaling of resources, and business venture initiation in the presence of risk are almost completely ignored.

As entrepreneurship education strives to enhance its impact on all three constituencies, a key imperative is, therefore, to remedy the deficiency identified with respect to initiator-oriented knowledge and skill areas. At the same time, in making the case for entrepreneurship education it is important not to forget that it is education which is universally germane, and lasts a lifetime. The knowledge and skills of entrepreneurship and entrepreneurial thinking are of benefit for any career path, not just for those leading to the start-up and development of business ventures. Additionally, the economic uncertainties and changes roiling both careers and job markets today are probably here to stay. In an environment of such unpredictable change, the capacity to initiate a business or take on a key role for an entrepreneurial initiative within a company is likely to be a very important "survival" asset—even for those who harbor no current interest in beginning a venture. The next chapters investigate three levels of knowledge and skill areas which are key to entrepreneurship and entrepreneurial thinking.

Endnotes

1. This chapter was adapted from the white paper by M. Kourilsky, "Entrepreneurship Education: Opportunity in Search of Curriculum," previously published in the *Business Education Forum*, October, 1995, and entered into the Congressional Record in 1997.

2. See Sahlman, W.A. & Stevenson, H.H. (1992). They also include a fourth component—the harvesting of the business, but that theme is not within the scope of this discussion.

3. See Slaughter (1995).

4. See Slaughter (1995).

5. See Kourilsky (1998) for a more in-depth discussion of the dimensions of entrepreneurial leadership.

Knowledge of Need, Skills of Success

The strategic linkage of two major trends—the increasingly entrepreneurial economy and the need for improved education in entrepreneurship—raises an important question. What specific types of knowledge and skills give young people the greatest opportunity to participate and succeed in this economy? This chapter addresses the question in detail.[1]

Entrepreneurship Education for All

One particular observation made in an earlier chapter deserves repeating. The knowledge and skills associated with entrepreneurship—and especially with entrepreneurial thinking and behaviors—are not limited in relevance only to business start-ups. Rather, they apply to all forms of creative ventures within the different sectors of the economy. These ventures could fall anywhere on an eclectic list ranging from the more familiar business start-up based on new products to the start-up of a new team or operating function within a private, public or not-for-profit organization.

Young people who aspire to join the "make-a-job" economy

(characterized by entrepreneurship) or the "take-a-job" economy (characterized by an increasing need for intrapreneurship) need to be equipped to initiate, advance and support entrepreneurial thinking and behaviors within a variety of contexts and different types of organizations.[2] In either case, they need the knowledge and skills to help them identify opportunity, marshal resources in the face of risk, and start a business. The education and training students receive to prepare them to start a business is of value for whatever role they ultimately play in our complex economy.

Secrets of the Pyramid

The following pyramid is helpful in framing the discussion of the knowledge and skills that are rapidly surging to the forefront of the extended intellectual asset profile required for success in the entrepreneurial economy. The pyramid is composed of three layers that progressively build toward entrepreneurship, entrepreneurial thinking and economic understanding.[3]

Figure 6.1: Pyramid Layers

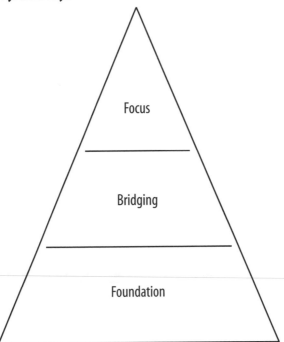

A Foundation of Fundamentals

The *Foundation* layer addresses fundamental knowledge and skills that are necessary antecedents for the higher-level learning and doing required for participation in the entrepreneurial economy. There are six major parts to this layer:

- Basic reading, writing and arithmetic.
- Seeing problems and coming up with ways to solve or fix them.
- Thinking about and using available information to produce solutions or answers.
- Deciding which solution or answer is the best among two or more choices.
- Seeing opportunities others may not see.
- Combining ideas or information in new ways.

Each item is important in its own right, and together they create a solid base for the development of other skills that prepare people for entrepreneurship.

Beginning with Basics. This layer begins with basic reading, writing and arithmetic, the essential elements of functional literacy for participating in the economy. Without a solid background in these areas, it is extremely difficult to become an entrepreneur. Instead of making a job, a person lacking these basics is significantly more likely to take a job, sometimes at the lowest levels in the economy.

Solving Problems. In addition to basic skills, this layer includes the separate but inter-related intellectual skill areas of *problem solving* and the *reasoning* associated with it. These two skill areas enable recognition and analytical dissection of problems, the use of logic to draw conclusions from available information, and the generation and implementation of plans to resolve or mitigate problems.

Teaching students how to solve problems is a major objective in many subjects, such as mathematics, science and business. Although the approach may differ for each subject, the recognition of problems and finding ways to solve them remains a significant focus. Successful entrepreneurs and entrepreneurial thinkers must have problem-solving skills, too.

Making Decisions. For most business and social problems, there are multiple solutions to consider. The difficulty is deciding which answer or choice is the best. Effective decision-making means goals and constraints are specified, alternative choices are considered in light of risks and benefits, and decisions are made after careful evaluation of the possibilities.

Developing these decision-making skills is crucial in order to avoid making decisions without sufficient consideration of goals, weighing of options and anticipation of consequences. Successful entrepreneurs are not simply lucky people. They are skilled and calculating decision makers.

Recognizing Opportunities. An important perspective embedded in the message of the pyramid is that *opportunity recognition*—an intellectual asset not typically recognized as foundational—is in fact a **key skill** of the base layer. In an economic environment characterized by rapid changes in technology, information, demographics and global competition, it is critical for young people to be able to see the opportunities for creative initiative behind the trends and within the gaps of their environment.[4]

It is equally important for them to be able to invoke the foundational skill of problem recognition and solving with a mindset that frames problems as opportunities, rather than as undesirable crises. Too often, problem solving is presented as a negative proposition rather than a positive experience which can expand possibilities. Entrepreneurial thinkers focus on the possibilities of each challenge rather than on its burdens.

Young people today are rarely exposed to the concept of opportunity recognition and, when exposed, are often given pre-identified opportunities. With very few exceptions, instructional programs fail to provide them with the education to learn to identify opportunities that exist within the context of problems and challenges.[5] Real education in entrepreneurship expands the possibilities for solving problems by turning negative viewpoints into positive potential.

Thinking Creatively. Combining ideas or information in new ways and conjuring connections between seemingly unrelated ideas or information is the essence of creative thinking. This type of thinking is included in the *Foundation* layer of the pyramid because it is so critical to entrepreneurship.[6]

An important distinction worth emphasizing is the relationship between creative thinking and opportunity recognition. Unconstrained creativity has been, and will continue to be, a seminal source of new ideas that enrich the human experience and environment. To maximize their effectiveness in an entrepreneurial economy, however, young people must also understand the difference between a creative idea—which may be quite intriguing and innovative—and an idea that addresses a viable opportunity for a sustainable entrepreneurial activity in their contemporaneous "here-and-now."

Building Bridges

The *Bridging* layer develops knowledge and skills in both business management and communication. These two components help young people make the connection from the *Foundation* layer to the resource clusters of today's entrepreneurial economy.

The resources needed for starting a business are many and varied. Perhaps most important are human resources. People need to be found to help the firm grow. Conditions must also be established for people to be as productive as possible at the new venture.

Of course, firms also need financial resources to hire workers and obtain the capital goods used for creation, production and distribution of products. Making the best use of these financial

resources is no small task. It is an on-going challenge that relies substantially on the problem solving, decision making and opportunity recognition previously described.

In our complex world, information and technology are valuable assets. An important challenge for entrepreneurs is to decide what information needs to be collected, where it is to be found and how it can be processed and shared to enhance growth for a start-up.

Mastering Management

The management knowledge and skill areas of the pyramid include the following six components:

- Making smart use of time.
- Budgeting money wisely.
- Managing others.
- Motivating others.
- Cooperating with others to meet team goals.
- Coming up with solutions or answers where everyone involved is better off.

What follows is a brief description of each area that helps aspiring entrepreneurs and others make the best use of scarce resources.

Using Time. Time is a precious commodity. There are only so many productive hours in the day, and most people feel the pressure of "not having enough time" to get everything accomplished that they want to do. Time management is a critical skill for entrepreneurs to develop if they are to accomplish their goals and be more productive.

Budgeting. The management of money resources is essential for both personal and business purposes. It is easy for individuals and firms to spend more money than they make, a course of action which may ultimately lead to bankruptcy. Learning about the management of cash flow to meet financial needs given expected expenditures and revenues is important to the success of any personal or business enterprise.

Managing. Businesses require individuals to coordinate and direct activities. This work involves developing a plan of action and making sure all workers are contributing to its success. Management tasks can be routine (e.g. handling day-to-day operations) or can require extraordinary innovation and insight to solve problems involving human, financial or technological resources. People can become good managers with education and training and make a valuable contribution to the entrepreneurial economy.

Motivating. A firm's leader and leadership team must motivate people in order to generate productivity and support within the organization. These individuals strive to create an environment in which all associates want to achieve success for the team because they perceive that their own personal well being and success are linked to the outcome. Start-up businesses rely heavily on the motivation of both the entrepreneur and the entrepreneurial team that helps the business to grow.

Motivation can be encouraged by extrinsic and intrinsic rewards. A major challenge is ascertaining what works to make people feel rewarded and recognized for doing a good job. In fact, when it comes to encouraging work effort, knowing what not to do may be just as important as knowing what to do to. Education can help people identify what may work best under different circumstances.

Cooperating. In modern business, people often team up on projects too large and complex for one person to handle. It follows, then, that the team members may collectively become responsible for the job.

But even though working together may constitute a large part of today's business environment, not everyone possesses the qualities needed to function well within a team framework. Therefore, they need sound and realistic educational experiences that let them experience working with others to achieve a common goal.

Negotiating. In the best of all worlds, people on all sides of an issue will perceive themselves as better off as a result of economic and other types of decisions. This means that in business, voluntary cooperation and agreement among people are preferable to authoritarian mandates. It tends to encourage broader participation and support.

Businesses often face problems finding solutions in situations where parties involved in the negotiation believe they ultimately will lose advantage or benefits. In most cases, creative thinking can be used to find solutions or answers where everyone is better off for the decision. Education can play a major role in developing the ability to negotiate solutions from which all parties derive benefits—or which at lease minimize unavoidable negative effects.

Communicating Better

A range of communication skills is essential for success in any endeavor. After all, when communication skills are poor, a great deal of confusion and misinformation can result. The communication component of the *Bridging* layer addresses the following five areas of this important topic:

- Listening to others.
- Giving presentations in front of others.
- Writing effectively.
- Communicating well in more than one language.
- Using e-mail, the Internet and other technology to find, send and receive information.

Listening. Being able to *listen well* is one key skill young people need to develop in order to work successfully with other people. It is important in two respects. First, it facilitates working with others in whatever roles they assume—as leaders, managers or coworkers. Second, listening closely to customers is necessary to garner valuable information and insights from their comments and complaints.

Presenting. On a daily basis, most communication is oral. So, equally important as listening to others is the ability to give *oral presentations* to individuals and groups. These presentations may simply involve providing information and responding to questions, or may be designed to persuade others to adopt a particular point of view. An inability to make such presentations has great potential for harming a business, either through internal miscommunications or externally through misstatements to customers or the public.

Writing. Simply knowing the basics of writing is not enough for success in business. Writing is a vital form of communication for employees, associates and customers. As with oral communication, writing may be informative and descriptive, or used to make a case for a project, product or position. People who want to start a business and make it prosper have to know how to make the most effective use of writing tools to convey their messages and advocate their positions.

Languages. As America's work force and customers grow increasingly diverse in background and heritage, communicating well in more than one language and understanding other cultures become increasingly valuable tools in helping to create wider markets.

Understanding other languages also helps us understand other cultures. A multi-lingual workforce can foster sensitivity to different needs and interests which, in turn, can help a firm do a better job of listening and communicating with customers and employees.

Technology. As rapid technological change is now a constant part of business life, young people need to develop and maintain a high level of comfort with it. In this way, they can participate more thoroughly and leverage the new tools that emerge through technological innovation.

In fact, the productivity of firms is closely linked to their employees' skills and knowledge in this arena. In today's environment, people must be able to acquire, process and exchange information using such technology as e-mail, the World Wide Web, business software applications and various electronic conferencing systems. They also must be comfortable dealing with the rate of change in this area and anticipating future technology directions.

Focusing on Success

The top layer of the knowledge and skills pyramid—the *Focus* layer—addresses the specific knowledge and skill areas required of young people to engage productively in either the "make-a-job" or "take-a-job" sectors of the entrepreneurial economy.

There are two major components to this layer. The first emphasizes the practical entrepreneurship skills people need most to start a business. The second covers the understanding of economic concepts of importance to entrepreneurs.

Effective Entrepreneurship

The entrepreneurship components of this layer are:

- The ability to tell the difference between good and bad opportunities.
- Reading and making sense of a business plan.
- What it takes to start a business.
- Accounting or record-keeping.
- Selling or advertising a good or service.
- How to decide what price to charge for a good or service.

These six items are major contributors to entrepreneurial effectiveness for those who enter any sector of the economy.

Assessing Opportunity. This first element emphasizes the importance of basing an entrepreneurial venture on an idea or opportunity that targets a realistic market niche capable of supporting the venture over time.[7] In addition to recognizing opportunities (an element of the *Foundation* layer previously discussed), this element requires the *evaluation of market opportunities* and the distinguishing of solid from marginal ones.

The linkage of this focus skill to a foundation skill gives special emphasis to a more general observation. The probability of successful use of the knowledge and skills outlined in the *Focus* layer to participate in the entrepreneurial economy is highly dependent on the quality of the underpinnings from both the *Bridging* and the *Foundation* layers.

Making a Business Plan. Well-constructed blueprints help entrepreneurial ventures or functions succeed in their niche markets. These game plans must test well for reality and define a compelling "value proposition" for their target customers or users—value based on actual benefits customers perceive they will derive from the features of the proposed service or good.

The plans should also reflect an on-going commitment to quality of production and the delivery of services or products to the complete satisfaction of their users. The knowledge and skills required for effectiveness in these areas include being able to read (or listen to) and to analyze critically entrepreneurial venture plans or business plans. Such capabilities also presume an understanding of what is needed in such plans to chart the course of the proposed ventures and to provide an acceptable basis for assessing their prospects for success.

Resources. Marshaling key resources—especially start-up capital and an initial team of talented associates—is one of the most challenging hurdles for initiating any kind of entrepreneurial function or venture. For the most part, these are resources over which one has neither direct ownership nor authority, at least at the outset.

Furthermore, these resources must be located and their commitment somehow secured for a proposition whose success cannot be guaranteed. This element drives an important knowledge requirement: young people must understand "what it takes" to start a business. This includes the spectrum of tangible resources (money, space, supplies ...) and intangible resources (time, labor, expertise, quality control ...) needed to start and operate a venture. Understanding is maximized if young people learn where such resources are most likely to be found, and discover the options for committing them to uncertain propositions whose objectives carry risk.

Accounting. Resources must be tracked and managed, and one basic skill used to accomplish this task is accounting and record-keeping. Learning how to make the best use of these tools allows people to monitor the employment of resources so they can be effectively used for the growth of the business. Accounting systems are also critical for measuring how a new venture is doing.

Selling. Entrepreneurial ventures are not successful unless they have a team with an extraordinary ability to sell to their target customers and users. The team must be able to persuade potential customers to exchange something of value, such as money or time, for products or functions. Advertising and promotion are knowledge and skill areas individuals need to draw on as they try to convey a passion for the products and services of the business.

Pricing. The degree to which their advertising and promotion skills translate into successful selling is also a function of young people's understanding of how to price products for their target markets. Entrepreneurs must be able to price their products taking into account such factors as market demand, competitors' pricing, production and operating costs, and desired profit margin. They must also construct effective messages that communicate benefits of the product relative to its price.

Essential Economics

To become entrepreneurs and be entrepreneurial in their thinking, young people must also understand the vital linkages between entrepreneurship and the underlying mechanisms and environment of a market economy. These are linkages that the *Focus* layer seeks to illuminate through its complementary emphasis on economics. There are five knowledge and skill areas in the economic component of this layer:

- Knowing that when you make a decision to do something, you give up your second-best choice.
- The role of supply and demand in the market.
- Knowing the role of government in business.
- Understanding how money can lose value over time (due to inflation).
- Knowing how to compete in a worldwide economy.

Each one gives aspiring entrepreneurs insights into how the economy works and how its functions interact with entrepreneurship.

Real Cost. One of the fundamental precepts of economics is that any time a decision is made there is an "opportunity cost." In making a decision, a person gives up the opportunity to select the next best alternative. What was given up is considered the measure of the real cost of that decision.

Entrepreneurs continually make decisions as they adjust their business to meet market variations, such as changes in consumer demand, costs or competition. For each decision, they must evaluate whether the benefits are greater than the opportunity cost. Young people can learn how to recognize this cost and factor it into their decision-making. In doing so, they will come to appreciate the relevance of economic reasoning to successful decision-making for an entrepreneurial venture.

Supply and Demand. Prices are determined in competitive markets through the interaction of supply and demand. Suppliers try to sell their products to consumers at the price that maximizes their profits. Consumers, wanting to maximize the value of their money, tend to buy less at higher prices. It is the interaction of the conflicting perspectives of buyers and sellers that establishes the market price for a product and how much of that product will be sold.

Understanding how markets work often is a mystery to those uneducated in basic economics. As a consequence, people may complain about the outcomes from a market because they view a resulting price as either too high or too low. In some cases, government intervention is sought to mitigate the effects of market outcomes without a full understanding of the broader economic consequences of such interventions. Such lack of awareness may result in policies that hinder entrepreneurship.

Government. At the federal, state and local levels, government plays a major role in our market economy. Its many activities include collecting taxes; spending funds on public programs; regulating commerce; providing a court system which helps enforce contracts; and supporting measurement standards. These functions can be alternatively beneficial or harmful to business formation and operation, depending on the context.

The entrepreneur needs to understand what government can do for good or ill to affect business operations. The enforceability of contracts is a key requirement for successful venture initiation growth. Many businesses also rely on the government's stabilization of measurement standards. On the other hand, the way certain taxes are levied can change the way a business operates. Some business regulations may tend to stifle entrepreneurship and raise the cost of doing business. Attempts to control prices historically have often led to market shortages.

Inflation. A major problem with high inflation is the resulting serious distortion of the value of money. This distortion makes decision-making more difficult because it is hard to calculate the costs and benefits of an economic decision. It also tends to erode the value of assets. This problem area is especially challenging for entrepreneurs. They need to know how to take the inflation factor into account in most aspects of their ventures including the selling of their products, the purchasing of resources and the general operation of their businesses.

Global. In today's global environment, young people must understand the skills and knowledge areas that will enable them to compete in a worldwide economy. The modern venture is operating in a world with increasingly fewer boundaries, a trend that demands unflagging and timely attention to the rapid oscillations of foreign and domestic markets. The changes in these markets affect many considerations, such as competition, pricing and innovation. At the same time, they represent both expanded opportunities and heightened risk for businesses.

In natural succession to this chapter's discussion of the knowledge and skills for entrepreneurship and entrepreneurial thinking, it is now time to examine survey findings on their relative importance and preparation.

Endnotes

1. For a more in-depth discussion of these points, see Kourilsky (1998). This white paper was developed on behalf of America's Promise—The Alliance for Youth, a national not-for-profit organization initiated under the leadership of General Colin Powell, USA (Ret.).

2. See Kourilsky (1998). See also Pinchot (1985) or Schneider, Teske, and Mintrom (1995) for an analysis of entrepreneurial activity within corporations or government.

3. This pyramid was introduced in Kourilsky (1998). The layering of the pyramid and the capability components emphasized at each layer reflect both synthesis and extension of inputs from many sources. These sources include publications of national standards in business education and economics, and relevant books (including Meszaros and Siegfried, 1997, and O'Neill, 1997). Other sources consulted were the SCANS report, the Work Keys initiative of the American College Testing (ACT) organization, a needs assessment of the member businesses of the Entrepreneur Of The Year® Institute, the Search Institute Youth Survey on behalf of America's Promise, national Gallup surveys commissioned by the Kauffman Center for Entrepreneurial Leadership, and papers and session outcomes from the first national School-to-Entrepreneurship Orientation Conference.

    The pyramid's knowledge and skill areas were also discussed with leaders from national organizations which focus on entrepreneurship education, economic education, or youth development. These organizations included the National Council on Economic Education (NCEE), the Foundation for Teaching Economics (FTE), Junior Achievement, the Calvin K. Kazanjian Foundation, the Society of Economic [and entrepreneurship] Educators (SEE), the Foundation on Economic Trends, Bell Atlantic New Jersey Office of the President, the Court Appointed Special [Child] Advocates (CASA), and the America's Promise/Alliance for Youth.

4. See Kourilsky (1995) and Kourilsky (1998) for further discussion.

5. See Kourilsky (1990) for a further discussion of classroom practices; see Kourilsky and Carlson (1997) and van der Kuip (1998) for more on exceptions.

6. See Kuratko and Hodgetts (1998), Miner (1997), or Chun (1997).

7. The terms "market" and "customers" are used to suggest not only the more traditional interpretation related to potential purchasers of goods or services in a market economy, but also to include the broader interpretation of potential "customers" or "users" of any forms of goods or functional services, including those that may be provided internally by an operating unit of an existing organizational framework, such as a communications group, an integration testing and quality assurance department, a research and evaluation unit, or a floating office assistant pool.

Multiple Perspectives, Important Implications

The previous chapter outlined the knowledge and skills young people need to become successful entrepreneurs and entrepreneurial thinkers. In this chapter, these knowledge and skills are analyzed from the perspectives of three different groups: youth, college students, and business leaders.[1] The findings have important implications for the conduct of entrepreneurship education.

Surveying Youth

The first group surveyed was high school youth.[2] The objective was to find out how they rated the *importance* of each knowledge or skill in high school education. For comparison purposes, the question was posed in two ways. First, youth were asked about the importance of the knowledge or skill for *starting a business*. They were then questioned about the importance of the knowledge or skill for *working for a business*.

Expectations. The first hypothesis was that in most cases, the importance of an item would be rated differently for starting a business versus working for a business. Youth were expected to rate the importance of most items significantly higher for starting a business.

The rationale for this hypothesis centers on the notion of an entrepreneurial attitude. If people believe they will start their own business—or even if they think others will be starting one—then they are more likely to rate a knowledge or skill as more important because there is a stronger need to know. Personal accountability becomes more pressing when someone starts his or her own business and is directly responsible for making it successful.

If a person does not possess a particular knowledge or skill, then the business could fail—or so the thinking might go.

By contrast, consider the probable attitude toward particular knowledge or skills if people believe they will work for someone else. In this case, they may see themselves as employees who are not directly responsible for the success or failure of the business. They may therefore think they need to know significantly less, finding it is easier to imagine that others (managers, directors or owners) require certain capabilities, but not necessarily employees. In the take-a-job situation, there is the tendency in the eyes of many to perceive less need for personal accountability with respect to certain knowledge and skills.

Preparation. Youth perspectives were also sought on the quality of the educational *preparation* high school graduates receive for each knowledge or skill. This information would be valuable for identifying the knowledge and skill areas for which youth thought they were better or more poorly prepared.

Employing Business Leaders

It is not enough to survey only youth on the importance and preparation questions, however. On many items, they may lack sufficient background or experience to make a realistic assessment. So, although youth opinions were of prime interest, the survey was expanded to examine how closely they match the opinions of those who may be more informed, or have a broader view of knowledge and skills issues. Business leader responses can also illuminate perspectives of those who may ultimately be hiring many of these youth.

To provide this contrast, a national sample of business leaders, randomly selected from Dun and Bradstreet lists of all businesses in the nation, was surveyed. Approximately half were located at small businesses (fewer than 50 employees) and the other half at larger ones.

In most cases, the respondent interviewed was the most senior leader at the company who made hiring decisions—the individual who should know the most about the job characteristics and educational background required of high school graduates the company might hire.[3]

Contrasts. The working hypothesis on the importance questions was the same as that stated for youth, for largely the same reasons. Business leaders were expected to rate most knowledge and skill areas as more important for someone starting a business and less important for someone working for a business.

The response of business leaders to the preparation question, however, was expected to be radically different from that of youth. Here it was suspected that business leaders would give schools lower marks than would youth on the quality of preparation of high school graduates.

The basis for this hypothesis is that business leaders have long been critical of the general quality of schooling and of the education of high school graduates. Numerous business leaders have called for reform in education to improve learning and better prepare students for the job market.[4] It was anticipated that this general criticism would be reflected in low ratings of preparation on most of the study's knowledge or skill items—certainly when compared to the perceptions of youth.

Going to College

Another educational dimension was added to the survey work by asking college students to assess the same list of 28 knowledge and skill items administered to youth.[5] One major change was made, however, for this evaluation. Instead of asking college students to rate the importance and preparation of items for high school graduates, we asked them to rate their importance and preparation *for college graduates.*

Underlying this approach was the belief that the knowledge

and skill areas needed to prepare people for entrepreneurship apply equally to education at both pre-college and college levels. College graduates need the same knowledge and skills as high school graduates if they are to participate fully in the entrepreneurial economy. Although examples used and teaching depth might differ, the knowledge and skill areas needed are substantially the same.

College students were also asked to rate the importance of a knowledge or skill in two ways: for starting a business and for working for a business. For reasons similar to those previously cited, it was anticipated there would be major differences in the importance ratings for the two situations. The same hypothesis was adopted for this group as for the other: items would be rated as more important for people to know if they are starting a business than if they are working for someone else.

On the preparation issue, it was expected that college students would be similar to youth in their orientation. It also was likely that the sheer quantity of time college students had spent in school would tend to elicit fairly positive evaluations of the quality of their preparation.

Contrasting Views

To contrast the views of college students with those of business leaders, another group of business leaders was surveyed. They were asked for their evaluation of the importance of each knowledge and skill item and the quality of preparation college graduates had received in each.

The same methodology was used to collect data from the national sample of business leaders judging college graduates as was used to gather data from business leaders evaluating high school graduates. The new sample was also an approximately evenly divided mix of business leaders from small and large firms. Again, the people sought for the interviews were the most senior executives hiring college graduates for their firms.[6]

On the importance issue, it was expected that business leaders' perceptions with respect to college graduates would be about the same as those of business leaders hiring high school graduates: both groups would give more importance to skills needed for starting a business than for working for a business. It was also expected that their thinking would be about the same as that of college students, and in most cases, of youth.

The major differences between the views of college students and those of the business leaders who hire college graduates would be their perspectives on preparation. On most items, it was expected that business leaders would be significantly less impressed with the education students received in college than would be the students themselves.

The rationale for this position was linked to the anticipation that college students, lacking business experience, would tend to overstate how well prepared they were with respect to a knowledge or skill—especially for starting a business. Having personally experienced many ill-prepared graduates from colleges, however, business leaders would likely be more critical of their preparation.

Analyzing the Big Picture

Each group was surveyed on all 28 knowledge and skill areas important to entrepreneurship and entrepreneurial thinking. To simplify the analysis, first presented are overall results showing the average response across all items on the survey. A later section reports average responses for the knowledge and skill areas in each of the *Foundation, Bridging* and *Focus* layers of the pyramid highlighted in the last chapter. The Appendix offers item-by-item results for more details about responses than can be provided by the overall or layer averages.[7]

Importance. The next table shows that slightly more than two-thirds of youth thought the overall set of knowledge and skills were extremely important for high school graduates if they were *starting a business.*[8] By contrast, less than half of youth rated the skills as extremely important for *working for a business.* The 19-point difference supports the initial hypothesis and suggests that youth view these knowledge and skill areas as significantly more important when thinking about entrepreneurship than when considering employment.

TABLE 7.1: Knowledge and Skill Areas for Entrepreneurship and Entrepreneurial Thinking: Overall

	Rating of Importance and Preparation for:			
	High School Graduates		College Graduates	
	Youth (n=1,032)	Business Leaders (1,312)	College Students (603)	Business Leaders (601)
	%	%	%	%
Overall (28 items)				
Extremely important for:				
Starting own business	67	73	73	70
Working for a business	48	42	48	43
Good preparation in school	62	24	66	46

On the importance question, the views of business leaders who might hire youth were about the same as those of youth. Business leaders were more likely to think the knowledge and skills were extremely important for high school graduates starting a business than for those working for someone else. The 31-point difference in ratings clearly supports the hypothesis for this group.

The same outcomes are seen at the college level in the responses of college students and of the business leaders who might hire college graduates. For college students, there is a gap of 25 percentage points between their ratings of importance for people starting a business and people working for someone else. A similar spread of 27 percentage points is seen for business leaders evaluating college graduates.

In sum, the results discussed so far suggest that all the groups have significantly higher perceptions of the importance of developing knowledge and skill areas when they are to be used for starting a business rather than working for someone else. The potential educational implication of these results is profound and will be addressed at the conclusion of this chapter.

Preparation. Youth believed that the preparation they received with respect to the knowledge and skills that equip them for entrepreneurship and entrepreneurial thinking was adequate. The evidence suggests, however, that they may over-estimate their preparation. In past studies, major deficiencies were found in the basic knowledge of entrepreneurship exhibited by youth.

Perhaps most telling on the issue is the response of business leaders to the preparation question. Only about a quarter of the business leaders surveyed thought there was adequate preparation of high school graduates in the study's knowledge and skill areas. In fact, there is a 38 percentage-point difference in the responses of youth and business leaders on the preparation question. In the minds of business leaders who are likely to hire high school graduates, the educational system has not prepared those graduates for entry into the entrepreneurial economy.

College. This critical assessment is not limited to high school. A similar divide is seen between college students and the business leaders who might hire college graduates. Two-thirds of college students think college graduates have good preparation in knowledge and skill areas that prepare them for entrepreneurship and entrepreneurial thinking. Business leaders were less impressed. Fewer than half of them thought college graduates had good preparation.

Looking at Layers

Overall results can mask interesting differences in subgroup results. To reveal such differences, the groupings of knowledge and skill areas corresponding to the *Foundation, Bridging* and *Focus* layers (described in the last chapter) were analyzed. Table 7.2 details the elements of the three groupings.

Anticipations. The same hypotheses about importance and preparation that were confirmed in the overall analysis were also conjectured for the layer analyses. Within each layer, a significant gap was predicted between the perceived importance of knowledge and skill areas for starting a business and for working for someone else. The thought of starting a business again was expected to make people see the more immediate need to learn a particular knowledge or skill area, regardless of its classification with respect to the *Foundation*, *Bridging* and *Focus* layers.

It was also believed that within each layer there would continue to be serious perception gaps, relative to preparation, between youth and college students on the one hand and business leaders on the other hand. Business leaders would still be highly critical of the quality of knowledge and skill education for each of the layers independently. Similarly, students would still rate their education higher within each layer—again in large part because of their limited job or business experience upon which to base a realistic assessment.

The preparation question, however, begged the question of whether the size of the responses varied by layer. It was suspected that the highest rating for preparation might be found in the *Foundation* layer. Because it contains basic knowledge and skills that are the focus of general education, youth or college students might be expected to believe they were well-prepared in these areas. For the same reason, business leaders would probably rate the preparation higher in this layer, too.

Analogously, the lowest rating for preparation was expected for the *Focus* layer, whose knowledge and skill areas are more specialized and often require coursework for any degree of proficiency. Many youth or college students might rate themselves lower in these areas than they would for the more general knowledge and skill areas of the *Foundation* or *Bridging* layers because of heightened sensitivity to lack of education or training. In fact,

TABLE 7.2: Layers of Knowledge and Skill Areas for Entrepreneurship and Entrepreneurial Thinking

Foundation Layer

1. Basic reading, writing and arithmetic
2. Seeing problems and coming up with ways to solve or fix them
3. Thinking about and using available information to produce solutions or answers
4. Deciding which solution or answer is the best among two or more choices
5. Seeing opportunities other may not see
6. Combining ideas or information in new ways

Bridging Layer

Management Component

7. Making smart use of time
8. Budgeting money wisely
9. Managing others
10. Motivating others
11. Cooperating with others to meet team goals
12. Coming up with solutions or answers where everyone involved is better off

Communications Component

13. Listening to others
14. Giving presentations in front of others
15. Writing effectively
16. Communicating well in more than one language
17. Using e-mail, the Internet and other technology to find, send and receive information

Focus Layer

Entrepreneurship Component

18. The ability to tell the difference between good and bad opportunities
19. Reading and making sense of a business plan
20. What it takes to start a business
21. Accounting or record-keeping
22. Selling or advertising a good or service
23. How to decide what price to charge for a good or service

Economics Component

24. Knowing that when you make a decision to do something, you give up your second-best choice
25. The role of supply and demand in the market
26. Knowing the role of government in business
27. Understanding how money can lose value over time (due to inflation)
28. Knowing how to compete in a worldwide economy

analysis of the survey data on course taking showed that only a minority of high school or college students took courses in entrepreneurship or economics. The survey data also showed that students gave themselves low self-ratings in their knowledge and understanding of starting a business.[9]

Findings. The results in the next table confirm the first hypothesis for the layer analysis. The data show a great divide between the ratings of importance for starting a business and for working for someone else, across all sample groups. At the *Foundation* layer, the percentage-point gaps are 15 for youth, 28 for business leaders (in the youth survey), 21 for college students, and 25 for their business leaders (in the college survey). For the *Bridging* layer, the differences are also substantial and range from 13 to 20 points, depending on the group.

The greatest divide is in the *Focus* layer, where there are percentage-point gaps of 28 for youth, 42 for the corresponding business leaders, 38 for college students, and 40 for the corresponding business leaders. The differences are almost double those of the equivalent comparisons for the *Foundation* and *Bridging* layers.

Why there are such significant differences in the *Focus* layer? These results are perhaps most directly attributable to the fact that the knowledge and skill areas of the *Focus* layer deal directly with entrepreneurship and economics. People are more likely to consider these specialized areas of extreme importance for starting a business and less likely to think of them as being important (or perhaps even relevant) when working for someone else.

The paradox is that the *Focus* layer knowledge and skills are no less important for those who will work for someone else than for those who intend to start a business. There are strong arguments to support how essential these knowledge and skill areas are for **every** high school and college student, independent of his or her intention to become or not to become an entrepreneur. Exposure to the concepts of the *Focus* layer develops entrepreneurial thinking

TABLE 7.3: Knowledge and Skill Areas for Entrepreneurship and
Entrepreneurial Thinking: By Layer

| | Rating of Importance and Preparation for: | | | |
| | High School Graduates | | College Graduates | |
	Youth (n=1,032)	Business Leaders (1,312)	College Students (603)	Business Leaders (601)
	%	%	%	%
A. Foundation Layer (6 items)				
Extremely important for:				
Starting own business	68	77	77	75
Working for a business	53	49	56	50
Good preparation in school	72	28	80	51
B. Bridging Layer (11 items)				
Extremely important for:				
Starting own business	63	67	68	63
Working for a business	50	47	53	48
Good preparation in school	64	25	68	43
C. Focus Layer (11 items)				
Extremely important for:				
Starting own business	71	76	77	74
Working for a business	43	33	39	34
Good preparation in school	54	20	57	46

and behavior of value to everyone who wants to achieve success in their chosen work—whether that work lies in the "make-a-job" sector or the "take-a-job" sector.

The data also confirmed the second supposition that youth and business leaders, or college students and business leaders, have differing perspectives on the degree of preparation. Across all three layers, there is a large divide between the higher rating of youth and the lower rating of business leaders. For youth and business leaders, the differences are 34–44 percentage points. For college students and business leaders, the gaps are 11–29 percentage points.

For both youth and college students, the gap narrows somewhat at the *Focus* layer. But that narrowing occurs primarily because more youth and college students indicate they are ill-prepared in their knowledge and skill areas. Youth gave themselves a preparation-by-school rating of 72 for the *Foundation* layer, 64 for the *Bridging* layer, and only 54 for the *Focus* layer. Among college students, the rating dropped from 80 at the *Foundation* layer, to 68 at the *Bridging* layer, and to 57 at the *Focus* layer. These results also support a third hypothesis about the expected fall in the school preparation ratings from the *Foundation* to the *Focus* layer.[10]

At the *Focus* layer, it is almost a 50-50 proposition whether youth or college students think they have good preparation. These doubts are consistent with earlier findings that most youth and college students receive limited direct education in entrepreneurship and that many express a lack of confidence in their ability to start a business.[11]

Analyzing Components

Within both the *Bridging* and *Focus* layers, subsets of knowledge and skill areas are organized into components. In the *Bridging* layer, there is a management component and a communications component. The *Focus* layer has an entrepreneurship component and an economics component. Several major differences in the response profiles for the importance questions are revealed when the results are analyzed by components.

In the *Bridging* layer, the management component has an average importance rating across the four sample groups of 75 per-

**TABLE 7.4: Knowledge and Skill Areas for Entrepreneurship
and Entrepreneurial Thinking: By Component**

	Rating of Importance and Preparation for:			
	High School Graduates		College Graduates	
	Youth (n=1,032)	Business Leaders (1,312)	College Students (603)	Business Leaders (601)
	%	%	%	%
A. Bridging: Management (6 items)				
Extremely important for:				
Starting own business	71	79	76	75
Working for a business	54	54	52	56
Good preparation in school	62	20	62	37
B. Bridging: Communications (5 items)				
Extremely important for:				
Starting own business	54	53	58	49
Working for a business	47	39	54	40
Good preparation in school	67	31	74	51
C. Focus: Entrepreneurship (6 items)				
Extremely important for:				
Starting own business	76	84	83	83
Working for a business	45	35	39	36
Good preparation in school	52	19	52	47
D. Focus: Economics (5 items)				
Extremely important for:				
Starting own business	65	65	69	63
Working for a business	40	31	39	31
Good preparation in school	58	20	63	46

113

cent, for *starting own business*. The corresponding average importance rating for the communication component is 54 percent. Why the difference?

The explanation lies primarily with two items that pull down the communication average. Only about 20 percent of each group thought communicating well in another language was extremely important for starting a business. Also, only about 53 percent in each group thought using e-mail, the Internet and other technology to find, send or receive information was extremely important for starting a business.

Both response percentages are unexpected. The low rating for the communications component's technology item may suggest a lack of awareness of how profoundly this knowledge and skill area is impacting opportunities for starting or expanding ventures.[12]

In the *Focus* layer, the entrepreneurship component is thought of as more important than the economics component for starting a business. The average rating across groups for the entrepreneurship items was 82 percent compared to only 66 percent for the economics items.

The explanation for this difference probably has to do with the more readily apparent immediacy and practicality of entrepreneurship over economics when thoughts turn to venture initiation. It is to be expected, for example, that knowing "what it takes to start a business" is likely to be thought of as more important for entrepreneurship than knowing "the laws of supply and demand."

Drawing Conclusions

The results discussed in this chapter reveal that across all layers and sample groups, there is a higher knowledge and skill expectation for people who are going to start a business than for people who will be working for somebody else. Because instruction in

our educational system is largely oriented toward students with the "take-a-job" mindset, there is a corresponding subliminal "lowering of the bar" with respect to the perceived standards of knowledge and skill competencies.

Concomitantly, the business/entrepreneur community's views of student preparation by their schools are uniformly lower than those of students. This disparity is independent of ratings for individual areas. Misperceptions among youth and college students about their degree of preparation for entrepreneurial activity directly affect them and the nation. They result in fewer businesses being started successfully because young people simply are not well-prepared to initiate a venture even if so disposed. The unrealistic assessment of knowledge and skills also leads to loss of valuable job opportunities, foregone income and under-utilization of intellectual and creative resources that could help both the entrepreneurial economy and its participants thrive.

There is a real opportunity embedded in these observations.

115

The overall level of education across all knowledge and skill areas could be significantly improved if educators were to adopt the perspective (and encourage students to do the same) that all students require the **quality of preparation** appropriate to eventually starting their own businesses. This perspective should be adopted regardless of students' ultimate career intentions.

The study results discussed in this chapter suggest a certain "higher quality mindset" associated by all groups with knowledge and skill areas that may be employed to pursue entrepreneurship and (by inference) to engage in entrepreneurial thinking. Invoking that higher quality mindset for classroom curricula and instruction *has the potential to raise learning standards for all high school and college students.*

Appendix 7-A

Knowledge and Skill Areas for Entrepreneurship and Entrepreneurial Thinking

	Rating of Importance and Preparation for:			
	High School Graduates		College Graduates	
	Youth (n=1,032)	Business Leaders (1,312)	College Students (603)	Business Leaders (601)
	%	%	%	%
1. Basic reading, writing and arithmetic				
Extremely important for:				
Starting own business	82	89	83	84
Working for a business	76	82	80	81
Good preparation in school	93	38	92	61
2. Seeing problems and then coming up with a way to solve or fix them				
Extremely important for:				
Starting own business	76	84	85	83
Working for a business	55	51	60	53
Good preparation in school	70	23	78	44
3. Thinking about and using what information one knows to come up with solutions or answers				
Extremely important for:				
Starting own business	63	74	72	71
Working for a business	49	48	54	46
Good preparation in school	73	30	85	56
4. Being able to decide which solution or answer is the best among two or more choices.				
Extremely important for:				
Starting own business	66	74	73	71
Working for a business	52	47	51	45
Good preparation in school	74	31	81	53

Knowledge and Skill Areas for Entrepreneurship and Entrepreneurial Thinking (continued)

| | Rating of Importance and Preparation for: | | | |
| | High School Graduates | | College Graduates | |
	Youth (n=1,032)	Business Leaders (1,312)	College Students (603)	Business Leaders (601)
	%	%	%	%
5. Seeing opportunities others may not see				
Extremely important for:				
Starting own business	61	75	78	76
Working for a business	43	34	44	38
Good preparation in school	55	17	66	38
6. Combining ideas or information in new ways				
Extremely important for:				
Starting own business	60	66	71	62
Working for a business	41	34	49	35
Good preparation in school	65	29	79	55
7. Making smart use of time				
Extremely important for:				
Starting own business	71	87	80	85
Working for a business	59	71	61	67
Good preparation in school	68	19	70	38
8. Budgeting more wisely				
Extremely important for:				
Starting own business	88	94	93	94
Working for a business	55	46	40	47
Good preparation in school	45	14	37	30

Knowledge and Skill Areas for Entrepreneurship and Entrepreneurial Thinking   (continued)

| | Rating of Importance and Preparation for: | | | |
| | High School Graduates | | College Graduates | |
	Youth (n=1,032)	Business Leaders (1,312)	College Students (603)	Business Leaders (601)
	%	%	%	%
9. Managing others				
Extremely important for:				
Starting own business	67	80	80	77
Working for a business	37	41	38	48
Good preparation in school	57	12	55	28
10. Motivating others				
Extremely important for:				
Starting own business	66	77	76	74
Working for a business	45	43	39	47
Good preparation in school	62	17	58	31
11. Cooperating with others to meet team goals				
Extremely important for:				
Starting own business	71	70	64	59
Working for a business	73	77	82	78
Good preparation in school	77	36	83	55
12. Coming up with solutions or answers where everyone involved is better off				
Extremely important for:				
Starting own business	61	66	61	60
Working for a business	52	45	52	47
Good preparation in school	64	23	70	39

Knowledge and Skill Areas for Entrepreneurship and Entrepreneurial Thinking (continued)

	Rating of Importance and Preparation for:			
	High School Graduates		College Graduates	
	Youth (n=1,032)	Business Leaders (1,312)	College Students (603)	Business Leaders (601)
	%	%	%	%
13. Listening to others				
Extremely important for:				
Starting own business	67	80	74	74
Working for a business	68	75	72	73
Good preparation in school	73	23	76	40
14. Giving presentations in front of others				
Extremely important for:				
Starting own business	55	58	59	52
Working for a business	44	26	54	29
Good preparation in school	73	28	82	58
15. Writing effectively				
Extremely important for:				
Starting own business	63	70	67	62
Working for a business	50	55	62	54
Good preparation in school	83	26	86	47
16. Communicating well in more than one language				
Extremely important for:				
Starting own business	32	13	22	13
Working for a business	26	10	21	9
Good preparation in school	57	21	41	29

**Knowledge and Skill Areas for Entrepreneurship and
Entrepreneurial Thinking** (continued)

	Rating of Importance and Preparation for:			
	High School Graduates		College Graduates	
	Youth (n=1,032)	Business Leaders (1,312)	College Students (603)	Business Leaders (601)
	%	%	%	%
17. Using e-mail, the Internet and other technology to find, send and receive information				
Extremely important for:				
Starting own business	55	43	69	44
Working for a business	46	29	62	33
Good preparation in school	49	57	87	83
18. The ability to tell the difference between good and bad opportunities				
Extremely important for:				
Starting own business	83	88	90	89
Working for a business	59	45	53	46
Good preparation in school	57	15	57	34
19. Reading and making sense of a business plan				
Extremely important for:				
Starting own business	73	82	79	78
Working for a business	55	39	52	40
Good preparation in school	58	17	59	47
20. What it takes to start a business				
Extremely important for:				
Starting own business	81	86	87	87
Working for a business	36	25	24	27
Good preparation in school	47	14	40	38

121

Knowledge and Skill Areas for Entrepreneurship and Entrepreneurial Thinking (continued)

	Rating of Importance and Preparation for:			
	High School Graduates		College Graduates	
	Youth (n=1,032)	Business Leaders (1,312)	College Students (603)	Business Leaders (601)
	%	%	%	%
21. Accounting or record-keeping				
Extremely important for:				
Starting own business	77	85	82	80
Working for a business	45	37	39	34
Good preparation in school	59	31	57	64
22. Selling or advertising a good or service				
Extremely important for:				
Starting own business	70	79	81	76
Working for a business	39	31	38	31
Good preparation in school	49	22	55	58
23. How to decide what price to charge for a good or service				
Extremely important for:				
Starting own business	72	86	80	86
Working for a business	35	35	28	37
Good preparation in school	39	15	42	40
24. Knowing that when you make a decision to do something, you give up your second-best choice				
Extremely important for:				
Starting own business	50	54	54	50
Working for a business	31	30	32	28
Good preparation in school	60	23	70	36

Knowledge and Skill Areas for Entrepreneurship and Entrepreneurial Thinking (continued)

	Rating of Importance and Preparation for:			
	High School Graduates		College Graduates	
	Youth (n=1,032)	Business Leaders (1,312)	College Students (603)	Business Leaders (601)
	%	%	%	%
25. The role of supply and demand in the market				
Extremely important for:				
Starting own business	72	79	83	78
Working for a business	42	35	43	38
Good preparation in school	60	26	70	62
26. Knowing the role of government in business				
Extremely important for:				
Starting own business	64	62	76	62
Working for a business	39	24	36	27
Good preparation in school	64	19	60	40
27. Understanding how money can lose value over time (due to inflation)				
Extremely important for:				
Starting own business	69	75	68	70
Working for a business	40	36	36	31
Good preparation in school	56	20	61	48
28. Knowing how to compete in a worldwide economy				
Extremely important for:				
Starting own business	69	57	64	53
Working for a business	47	30	50	32
Good preparation in school	50	14	56	44

123

Endnotes

1. For detailed analyses for underserved and advantaged youth, see Kourilsky and Kourilsky (1999a) and Kourilsky and Kourilsky (forthcoming).

2. Two groups of youth were surveyed about their views of skills needed by high school graduates. Youth from lower socioeconomic backgrounds were surveyed in spring 1998. In spring 1999, youth from middle to upper socioeconomic backgrounds were surveyed. For the first group, the sampling error was +/-3.5 percentage points at the 95 percent level of confidence. It was +/-3.1 percentage points for the second. The responses from both surveys were similar, so for the sake of parsimony in the book, we combined the responses.

3. Two groups of business leaders were surveyed about their views of high school graduates. The spring 1998 survey of business leaders asked questions about the needs of disadvantaged high school graduates. The spring 1999 survey asked business leaders the same questions about the needs of high school graduates from advantaged backgrounds. For the first group, the sampling error was +/-3.7 percentage points at the 95 percent level of confidence. For the second group of youth, it was +/-3.5 percentage points. Because similar responses were found from both surveys, their results were combined to avoid duplication.

4. For examples see Gerstner, Doyle, and Semerad (1994) or Olson (1998).

5. At the 95 percent level of confidence, the maximum expected range of the sampling error for the sample of 603 college students was +/- 4.0 percentage points.

6. At the 95 percent level of confidence, the maximum margin of sampling error for this college-oriented group of business leaders was +/-4.0 percentage points.

7. For survey data, see Kourilsky and Kourilsky (1999a) and Kourilsky and Kourilsky (1999b) whose results this appendix consolidates. Note that averages can mask some major differences within a set. For example, about nine in 10 youth thought that budgeting money wisely was extremely important, but only about three in 10 thought communicating well in another language was extremely important.

8. The overall and individual layer results were of most interest because they show the general patterns in the data that might be missed by focusing on a particular item. The overall and layer results also provide the most reliable data for testing our hypotheses because they are averages across multiple items. The item-by-item results, however, are also worth studying. They show the thinking of each group about a particular knowledge or skill area.

9. See Chapter 4.

10. There is only a minimal decline in the ratings of either group of business leaders across the layers. That decline probably is attributable to their ratings being relatively low to begin with for the *Foundation* layer and consequently having less downside potential for change.

11. See Chapter 4 for a discussion of these points.

12. College students, however, thought technology was more important. Among this group, 69 percent thought it was extremely important for starting a business. See the item tables in the chapter appendix.

Education for Today, Entrepreneurs for Tomorrow

In the 21st century, our economy will increasingly rely on entrepreneurship to stimulate economic growth, create jobs and develop new products and technologies. In this new era, entrepreneurial thinking and action in all forms will shape the character of American enterprise and guide its direction for the foreseeable future. From the launching of start-up businesses to the assumption of responsibility for opportunity recognition, leadership and change in existing organizations, entrepreneurial thinking will dominate.

Given this vision, a major challenge facing our society is the preparation of young people for the expanding world of entrepreneurial thinking and venturing. The years to come appear destined to be dominated by entrepreneurs and the entrepreneurial process—even more so than in the past century. We desperately need to give youth and young adults the knowledge and skills they need to equip them for this continuing evolution of the American business and organizational landscape.

So far, this book has addressed key aspects of that challenge by offering new insights about young people's interest in entrepreneurship, and their attitudes toward the role it will play in their lives. It further explored the obstacles hindering their pursuit of entrepreneurship and the key role education can play in fostering entrepreneurial thinking skills and attitudes.

Now it's time to highlight some of the major findings and recommendations suggested by the extensive national survey investigations which served as the foundation for *The E Generation*.

Showing Strong Interest

The desire to start a business is pervasive. Six to seven in 10 youth and young adults indicated they wanted to start their own businesses. About half of each group also said it is *likely* or *very likely* that they will act on their urge—convincing evidence that entrepreneurship is something they want to do. Furthermore, it is something they can succeed in doing if appropriate educational preparation is made available to overcome the obstacles in their paths.

Also encouraging is that the idea of starting a business does not appear to be a passing thought or idle speculation. Most of the youth and young adults surveyed had been thinking about it for some time. They also expected to start their business within a few years of completing their education in high school or college.

A major implication to be drawn from the survey evidence is that there is a large number of *actual* and *potential* entrepreneurs (and entrepreneurial thinkers) among our nation's youth and young adults. They constitute a resource pool that is prone to be overlooked—or at best, underestimated. It is this group, the E Generation, who is destined to shape the economic landscape and key organizations of the 21st century.

The E Generation clearly shows potential for making substantial contributions to the growth and development of our society. To fulfill that potential, however, the nation must focus on how best to tap into this entrepreneurial "mother-lode." Later in the chapter, we'll discuss ways of leveraging education to enhance the "mining" of this national resource of actual and potential entrepreneurs and entrepreneurial thinkers.

Helping Others

The profile of Generation E does not conform to popularized selfish stereotypes, such as being out to raise personal income and create wealth only for oneself. In fact, making a great deal of money was relatively poorly subscribed to on the list of key reasons for starting a business. The major reason cited for starting a business is one which has long been associated with the entrepreneurial spirit: a desire for independence. These young people want to be their own boss and take control of their lives. They also want the opportunity to make use of their skills and to master the challenge of starting a business.

Beyond personal reasons, however, our nation's young have another potentially strong (but only partially recognized) area of affinity to entrepreneurship. This generation sincerely wants to make a valuable contribution to society and to the communities in which they live. One important way they may be able to accomplish their goal is through entrepreneurship. To appreciate this option, however, they must make the connection between starting a business and helping the community.

Half of the connection has been made. Overwhelmingly, they think successful entrepreneurs have a responsibility to "give back" to the community. Where they need help is in making the other half of the connection: that entrepreneurship is an avenue for achieving the economic capacity to pursue philanthropic initiatives. Appropriate education can help this generation understand that forming new ventures and acting in entrepreneurial ways can be very effective approaches to assisting communities.

It is the merging of community development with self-development that will continue to distinguish Generation E from previous cohorts. Rather than attending to philanthropic considerations only after their ventures become profitable or are sold, the E Generation gives them priority even before launching their businesses.

Overcoming Obstacles

Initiating a venture is no easy task. Generation E may want to become entrepreneurs, but many obstacles can hinder their ability or propensity to act on those intentions. Such obstacles must be understood and addressed if the pool of aspiring youth and young adults are to join the ranks of future entrepreneurs—and if their inclination towards entrepreneurial thought and action is to be successfully encouraged.

First, the attitudes of many youth and young adults will need to be more "entre-initiating" if their interest in entrepreneurship is to ascend to the level of actual initiation of a venture. In other words, they have to have the stomach to "seize

the moment" and the entrepreneurial thought processes to deal with the trade-offs, issues and ambiguities of starting a business.

Second, interested youth and young adults will need to be prepared to overcome the key external roadblocks they perceive. When asked directly what they believed the greatest obstacles are to entrepreneurship, young people invariably mentioned the problems of obtaining financing. In the minds of many, the anticipated inability to secure financing makes entrepreneurship seem like an almost insurmountable challenge.

Third, young people also worry about "how to get started." Initiating a business appears to be an overwhelming task requiring too much time and energy, and in their minds is a huge personal commitment. The risks associated with a new venture and the fear of failure may stop many from taking action.

Compounding these problems is lack of cognitive self-confidence and the self-doubts such lack engenders. This perceived lack of know-how was suggested by the large percentage of young people who cited insufficient education and training as one of the barriers to entrepreneurship. Other survey responses revealed that many give themselves a low rating in their knowledge and understanding of how to start a business.

Educating for Success

Fortunately, all of these perceived obstacles can be mediated through education and training appropriately designed to prepare young people for the entrepreneurial economy of the 21st century. Such an education would help illuminate how to break down into manageable pieces and understand entrepreneurial processes such as recognizing opportunities, identifying target markets or securing funding for a venture. If youth and young adults are provided insights on how to maximize the probability of success and minimize the downside risks, they may be better positioned to overcome their fear of failure.

A good education and preparation for entrepreneurship has the potential to change the mindset that views starting a venture as "mission impossible." Ideally, it can be replaced by a mindset that perceives a mission replete with opportunities.

Young people already understand the importance of education for starting a business. The survey asked them to state what they thought has given them, or will give them, the most preparation for starting a business. For youth, the response that dominated all others was "education in school." Young adults also cited education, along with job experience most had obtained from already being in the workforce.

The problem is too few young people receive education that adequately prepares them for entrepreneurship. Fewer than four in 10 youth and young adults who wanted to start a business reported taking a high school course in either business or entrepreneurship. For those young adults who also attended college and were interested in starting a business, only about a third took a course in small business or entrepreneurship. Given these results, it is no wonder that most young people feel ill-prepared.

Of course, not all of the instruction needs to take place in the classroom. Education for entrepreneurship can also occur outside of school. Such external instruction could take place, for example, in conjunction with extracurricular or community projects associated with various public and private organizations. Developing partnerships between schools and business or social entrepreneurs; creating internships for students; using entrepreneurs as mentors and role models; and making wide use of community resources all foster the spirit and experiences of entrepreneurship sought by Generation E.

The nation experiences significant loss when aspiring entrepreneurs fail to get an education that helps them start businesses or helps them develop the skills to think in entrepreneurial terms for whatever work they do. The interests of youth may never be converted into action because they do not have sufficient knowledge and training to achieve their goals. As a consequence, there is less entrepreneurial thought capacity to invest in economic growth. The potential for new businesses and new job creation in the economy, in turn, is seriously diminished.

Making Versus Taking Jobs

Not all young people want to start a business. Why should it be important, then, for everyone to learn the knowledge and skills associated with becoming an entrepreneur? Simply stated: we strongly believe such an education can make all students more entrepreneurial in their thinking, regardless of whether they will eventually start their own business or work for someone else.

It does not matter whether young people expect to initiate

ventures in the "make-a-job" sector (entrepreneurship) or apply entrepreneurial thinking and creativity to existing organizations in the "take-a-job" sector (intrapreneurship). In either case, they will need the knowledge and skills to give them the best chance to survive and prosper in our increasingly entrepreneurial economy.

Most job-related or career education young people receive in their high school or college courses tends to prepare them for employment by someone else. There is insufficient attention given to entrepreneurial thinking and to the option of creating a job by starting a business. The result is that most young people follow traditional career paths into service, technical, professional and other occupation areas. Although this channeling is responsible for supplying much of our important employee functions (plumbers, office assistants, business managers, sales agents, lawyers, engineers, government officials and the like) it also encourages the perception that "other" organizations or people supply jobs. Young people think of themselves as working for someone else instead of connecting with their potential for creating their own jobs.

This "take-a-job" approach to education is especially restrictive for young people from lower socioeconomic backgrounds. They typically have fewer opportunities at home to learn about how business works and have less access to role models for entrepreneurship. Without the opportunity to learn what it takes to start and run a business, they may never even consider this as a viable possibility. Such lack of opportunity unnecessarily limits their vision of employment options and contributes to reduced expectations on their part for how they might participate productively in our economy.

Regardless of one's socioeconomic status, education in entrepreneurship provides excellent tools for creating alternatives in the event of a layoff or of irreparable dissatisfaction with current job opportunities. Knowing how to start a business gives people choices in dealing with any job situation—choices that they would most likely not have without such an education. With appropriate background and training, if members of the "take-a-job" workforce get laid off or want to leave a job, they know that finding another job is not their only option. They could work for themselves! Even if the entrepreneurship "card" is never played, knowing it exists gives people greater confidence and negotiating power in dealing with the vagaries of the traditional job market.

Developing Real Entrepreneurship Education

How important is entrepreneurship education? Its significance is underlined by the growth trends of our economy and our society's organizations, by the widespread interest of youth and young adults, and by the insistent signals of major deficiencies in their knowledge and skills. For such education to be effective, however, it must encourage entrepreneurial thinking and focus on the core attributes of real entrepreneurship: opportunity recognition, the marshaling of resources in the presence of risk, and the development of a new venture.

Unfortunately, the education most young people receive in the name of entrepreneurship gives little attention to these core issues. It focuses primarily on business management concepts more related to the operating functions of managers and executives than to the challenges and decisions faced by venture initiators.

What is usually overlooked in the teaching of entrepreneurship is that without opportunity recognition, marshaling resources in the presence of risk, and the creation of a business organization, there would be nothing to which to apply the principles of business management. Too much of the focus of instruction conducted today in the name of entrepreneurship is devoted to the management of operating functions, such as human resources, finance, marketing, selling and manufacturing. Students typically are not given the opportunity to experience personally and assume full responsibility for the creative activities, risks, uncertainties, and rewards of the entrepreneurial process. In those instances when such personal involvement is included, it is usually fatally diluted by external intervention and by group control.

Real entrepreneurship education is also important for all three constituencies of entrepreneurship and entrepreneurial thinking: the initiators, the development and support teams, and the stakeholders. To date, however, curricular impact has been largely confined to the latter two groups.

Economic education which integrates entrepreneurship issues does have a positive effect on economic/entrepreneurial literacy, which is key to the effectiveness and informed decision making of stakeholders. It helps create a constituency that understands the need for innovation in the economy. Without such a broad base of support for entrepreneurship, it is much less likely that the proper economic climate will exist for the fostering of new venture creation.

There are many nations throughout the world where entrepreneurship and its benefits are poorly understood. The stifling of entrepreneurship in many of these regions can in large measure be attributed to widespread lack of comprehension, encouragement and support. Both the general population and key decision makers in such areas are often poorly informed and/or have not bought in to the value entrepreneurship can bring to their economy and social objectives.

The development and support constituency also is deriving some benefit from business management education curricula and alternative approaches such as team building and cooperative learning. To enhance their chances of success in helping the initiators scale up both process and performance during a venture's growth phase, it is important that the dimensions of entrepreneurial leadership play a more central role in the education of this group.

It is the initiator group whose knowledge and skills garner the least attention in our country's instructional venues. Specific education and personal experience in core initiator areas are usually passed over in favor of instructional units that deal with generic attributes such as flexibility, tenacity and tolerance of ambiguity—often in concert with some discussion of the procedural aspects of a business start-up. Remedying this deficiency must be a key educational imperative if we are not to waste the entrepreneurial aspirations and motivation of our youth and young adults.

Coordinating Knowledge and Skills Sets

If youth and young adults are indeed to be prepared for successful participation in the entrepreneurial economy—whether they join the "make-a-job" or the "take-a-job" sector—attention must be devoted in their education to three coordinated sets of knowledge and skill areas. These sets can be viewed as layers of a pyramid that build toward the ultimate goals of entrepreneurship, entrepreneurial thinking and economic understanding.

Fundamental knowledge and skills are found in the *Foundation* layer. They are the prerequisite for the higher levels of understanding and activity that people need for participation in the entrepreneurial economy. These foundation knowledge and skill areas include reading, writing and arithmetic; problem solving; reasoning; decision making; and creative thinking. However, this base layer must also include the less familiar area of opportunity recognition, a cornerstone intellectual asset. It is key to making one's way amidst the oscillations of the entrepreneurial economy and to decoding the opportunities inherent in the problems one inevitably encounters.

The *Bridging* layer of the pyramid develops the knowledge and skill areas related both to business management and to communication, linking the *Foundation* layer attributes to the resource pools of the entrepreneurial economy. The first component covers the use and management of time, money and people resources in the various contexts of enterprise, as well as related motivation and negotiation skills. The communication component, which helps people understand others and express, exchange and process ideas and information, focuses on knowledge and skills such as listening; presenting; writing; communicating in or understanding foreign language; and using new technology.

The *Focus* layer at the top of the pyramid addresses the specific knowledge and skill areas that help young people make a productive contribution to the entrepreneurial economy in both "make-a-job" and "take-a-job" contexts. The first component includes key practical entrepreneurship skills people need for initiating and operating any kind of a venture. These include evaluating the prospects of various opportunities; analyzing business plans and start-up requirements; financial tracking and accounting; selling and advertising approaches; and pricing products. The second component enables understanding of the interaction effects between the fundamental mechanisms and issues of the market economy and those of entrepreneurship. It focuses on the basic ideas and concepts of economics that are particularly germane to entrepreneurs, such as opportunity cost, supply and demand, government regulation, inflation and global competition.

Although there are some 28 different knowledge and skill areas that make up the pyramid, the central message should not be lost amid the attention to its multiple layers and components. *Education for entrepreneurship and entrepreneurial thinking must be broad-based, drawing on many content areas.* It is not just about the "nuts and bolts" of starting or running a business. It is also about learning to recognize opportunity, make decisions, think creatively, lead people, leverage technology and understand how the economy works.

From economic as well as social perspectives, it is strategically important for our youth and young adults to be properly prepared to jump-start, move ahead and support entrepreneurial behaviors and thought models within a multiplicity of contexts and organizations. To accomplish this goal, their education must address a wide array of basic, connecting and specific knowledge and skill areas central to entrepreneurship and to entrepreneurial thinking.

Grading Courses and Curricula

The entrepreneurship education goals discussed so far will remain elusive so long as high school curricula continue their discrete and disjointed approach to this area. Today, little or no effort is made to integrate and draw connections for the student across courses in existing subject areas such as business and business management, personal finance, economics and even entrepreneurship. Like more traditional curricular domains (e.g. math and language arts), these discrete offerings need to be pulled together into sequences of integrated, in-depth courses in which entrepreneurship and entrepreneurial thinking are carried as anchoring and unifying themes. The component courses should be enriched to ensure that students receive instruction in the key knowledge and skill areas of the pyramid, and sequenced so their progression systematically reinforces and expands upon prior learning.

There is also a need for a capstone course in "advanced application" of entrepreneurship. It would review previous learning and related content, then focus on the specific knowledge and skills for identifying appropriate opportunities and gathering the resources to initiate for-profit or not-for-profit ventures which address those opportunities. Such a course would include mentoring and internship experiences at start-up businesses in local communities, and a chance for students to start real businesses. In this way, they could assume responsibility for the decision-making and the risks attendant upon such ventures.

The number of entrepreneurship courses at the post-secondary level has increased in the last few years. However, at the college level course sequences and related field activities that result in an entrepreneurship certificate of emphasis may significantly enhance the liberal arts experience. In general, if the themes of entrepreneurship and entrepreneurial thinking are included as focal points for the education of high school and college students, they will be better prepared for survival and meaningful contribution in the entrepreneurial economy of the 21st century.

Surveying Importance and Preparation

A central role has been suggested for the knowledge and skill areas necessary for entrepreneurship, entrepreneurial thinking and economic understanding. A natural target of investigation was to assess the perceptions of youth, young college adults and business leaders with respect to the importance of each of the 28 knowledge and skill areas—either for starting a business or for working for someone else. Also under scrutiny were the beliefs of the three groups about the preparation of youth and young adults in each knowledge/skill area. The survey responses produced several interesting and challenging findings.

Importance. In most cases, the importance of an item was rated significantly higher when youth, young college adults or business leaders considered its importance for starting a business compared with its importance for working for a business. The major reason suggested for these contrasting results is perceived personal accountability.

On the one hand, if people think they will start their own businesses—and by extension, if they are thinking about others starting their own businesses—they will tend to rate the importance of a knowledge or skill item higher because there is more perceived personal responsibility and accountability for the success of the business. On the other hand, if people think they (or others) will be working for someone else, there is less of a perception of personal responsibility and accountability and therefore less perceived need for mastering that knowledge or skill. The importance rating plunges in this latter instance.

Preparation. There is a major dichotomy between the views of youth and business leaders and between the perceptions of young college adults and business leaders about the quality of preparation high school and college graduates receive in the pyramid's 28 knowledge and skills areas for entrepreneurship and entrepreneurial thinking. Most youth think they receive adequate preparation in

141

school in these knowledge or skill areas, whereas most business leaders who will be hiring them do not. Similarly, young college adults perceive themselves to be better prepared by their educational institutions in these knowledge and skills than do the business leaders who hire college graduates.

Who is to be believed? Because the business leaders are the ultimate "customers" in the sense that they hire the youth and young adults in question, their opinions must carry more weight. The logical conclusion, then, is that there are significant deficiencies in the education of high school and college graduates. The educational system as it now operates has not prepared these graduates for successful participation in an entrepreneurial economy.

From these survey findings, a novel educational implication emerges. There appears to be a subliminal but substantial "raising of the bar" with respect to knowledge and skill expectations for people who are going to start a business, compared to expectations for people who intend to work for someone else. This apparent (make-a-job) "higher order mindset" effect could be used to raise the level of knowledge and skill learning across **all areas** by adopting the educational strategy to prepare all students at quality levels **consistent with** their having eventually to start their own businesses.

This strategy would apply to students regardless of their ultimate career intentions. More importance would be attached to the various knowledge and skill areas, and they would be more likely to be taught from a "make-a-job" perspective. To the extent that students also were successfully encouraged to adopt the proposed "make-a-job" attitude toward learning, they would take knowledge and skill areas more seriously and be more likely to invest the efforts necessary to learn them. Curriculum and instruction which taps into this (make-a-job) "double standard" could well elevate student acquisition of knowledge and skills "across the board" and create a higher de facto standard of learning.

Making Some Final Observations

Much of the economic, social and technological developments of the 21st century are expected to be driven by the entrepreneurial impetus of the E Generation. This expectation, however, is held hostage to the determination with which we choose to engage the issues raised in this book. We must remedy the obstacles identified for youth and young adult entrepreneurship, entrepreneurial thinking, and effective entrepreneurship education.

At the same time, it is important to keep the larger picture in mind. Entrepreneurship and entrepreneurial thinking are not just about starting businesses nor are they relevant only to aspiring initiators and development teams. They are profoundly important coping mechanisms that can help everyone deal with the hidden opportunities and unexpected changes of life. Indeed, exploration of the tensions and interplay between the "take-a-job" and "make-a-job" mindsets is—in the finest spirit of the liberal arts tradition—an important part of learning for all young people who seek insight into who they are and where they are going.

REFERENCES

Bernstein, D. (1992). *Better Than A Lemonade Stand: Small Business Ideas for Kids*. Hillsboro, OR: Beyond Words Publishing.

Brophy, D.J. (1997). "Financing the Growth of Entrepreneurial Firms." In D.L. Sexton and R.W. Smilor (eds.), *Entrepreneurship 2000* (pp. 5-27). Chicago, IL: Upstart Publishing.

Brown, C.M. (1999). *Nobody's Business But Your Own: A Business Start-Up Guide With Advice from Today's Most Successful Young Entrepreneurs*. New York: Hyperion.

Chun, J. (1997.) "Theory of Creativity: Two Creative Geniuses Reveal How to Think Out of the Box," *Entrepreneur*, 25(10), (October), 126-135.

Gerstner, L., Doyle, D.P., & Semerad, R.D. (1994). *Reinventing Education: Entrepreneurship in America's Public Schools*. New York: Dutton.

Isachsen, O. (1996). *Joining the Entrepreneurial Elite: Four Styles to Business Success*. Palo Alto, CA: Davies-Black Publishing.

Kent, C. (ed.). (1990). *Entrepreneurship Education: Current Developments, Future Directions*. New York: Quorum Books.

Kirchhoff, B.A. (1994). "Entrepreneurship Economics." In W.D. Bygrave (ed.), *The Portable MBA in Entrepreneurship* (pp. 410-439). New York: John Wiley & Sons.

Kourilsky, M.L. (1990). "Entrepreneurial Thinking and Behavior: What Role in the Classroom?" In C.A. Kent (ed.), *Entrepreneurship Education: Current Developments, Future Directions* (pp. 137-152). New York: Quorum Books.

Kourilsky, M.L. (1995). "Entrepreneurship Education: Opportunity in Search of Curriculum." *Business Education Forum,* 50(10), 11-15.

Kourilsky, M.L. (1998). "Marketable Skills for an Entrepreneurial Economy." White Paper. Kansas City, MO: Ewing Marion Kauffman Foundation.

Kourilsky, M.L. & Carlson, S.R. (1997). "Entrepreneurship Education for Youth." In D. Sexton and R. Smilor (eds.), *Entrepreneurship 2000,* (pp. 193-213). Chicago, IL: Upstart Publishing.

Kourilsky, M.L. & Kourilsky, G.N. (1999a). *Marketable Career Skills for Youth: Importance and Preparation.* Kansas City, MO: Ewing Marion Kauffman Foundation.

Kourilsky, M.L. & Kourilsky, G.N. (forthcoming). *Marketable Career Skills for Youth and Young College Adults: Importance and Preparation.* Kansas City, MO: Ewing Marion Kauffman Foundation.

Kourilsky, M.L. & Walstad, W.B. (1988). "Entrepreneurship and Female Youth: Knowledge, Attitudes, Gender Differences, and Educational Practices," *Journal of Business Venturing,* 13(1), 77-88.

Kuratko, D.F. & Hodgetts, R.M. (1998). *Entrepreneurship: A Contemporary Approach* (4th ed.). Ft. Worth: The Dryden Press.

Kushell, J. (1999). *The Young Entrepreneur's Edge: Using Your Ambition, Independence, and Youth to Launch A Successful Business.* New York: Villard Books.

Meszaros, B.T. & Siegfried, J.J. (1997). *Voluntary National Content Standards in Economics.* New York: National Council on Economic Education.

Miner, J.B. (1997). *A Psychological Typology of Successful Entrepreneurs.* Westport, CT: Quorum Books.

Morris, M.H. (1998). *Entrepreneurial Intensity: Sustainable Advantages for Individuals, Organizations, and Societies.* Westport, CT: Quorum Books.

National Federation of Independent Business. (1996). *Wells Fargo/NFIB Series on Business Starts and Stops.* Washington, DC: NFIB.

National Foundation for Women Business Owners (NFWBO). (1999). "Women-Owned Businesses Top 9 Million in 1999," *NFWBO Research Summary,* (May 11), 1.

O'Neill, H.F., Jr., (ed.). (1997). *Workforce Readiness: Competencies and Assessment.* Mahwah, NJ: Lawrence Erlbaum Associates.

O'Reilly, B. (1999). "What It Takes to Start A Startup," *Fortune* (June 7), 135-140.

Olson, L. (1998). *The School-To-Work Revolution: How Employers and Educators Are Joining Forces to Prepare Tomorrow's Skilled Workforce.* Cambridge, MA: Perseus Books.

146

Petzinger, T., Jr. (1999). *The New Pioneers: The Men and Women Who Are Transforming the Workplace and the Marketplace.* New York: Simon and Schuster.

Pinchot, G. (1985). *Intrapreneuring: Why You Don't Have to Leave the Corporation to Become an Entrepreneur.* New York: Harper and Row.

Sahlman, W.A. & Stevenson, H.H. (1992). *The Entrepreneurial Venture: Readings.* Boston, MA: Harvard Business School Publications.

Schneider, M., Teske, P. & Mintrom, M. (1995). *Public Entrepreneurs: Agents for Change in American Government.* Princeton, NJ: Princeton University Press.

Sharma, P. (ed.). (1999). *The Harvard Entrepreneurs Club Guide to Starting Your Own Business.* New York: John Wiley & Sons.

Slaughter, M.P. (1995). "Key elements that distinguish entrepreneurship." Internal memorandum. Kansas City, MO: Kauffman Center for Entrepreneurial Leadership, Ewing Marion Kauffman Foundation.

Small Business Administration. (1997). *Facts about Small Business.* Washington, DC: SBA.

Smilor, R.W. & Sexton, D.L. (eds.). (1996). *Leadership and Entrepreneurship.* Westport, CT: Quorum Books.

Stanley, T.J. & Danko, W.D. (1996). *Millionaire Next Door: The Surprising Secrets of America's Wealthy.* Atlanta, GA: Longstreet Press.

Stewart, W.H., Jr. (1996). *Psychological Correlates of Entrepreneurship*. New York: Garland Publishing.

Timmons, J.A. (1990). *New Business Opportunities: Getting to the Right Place at the Right Time*. Acton, MA: Brick House Publishing.

Timmons, J.A. (1999). *New Venture Creation: Entrepreneurship for the 21st Century* (5th ed.). Boston, MA: Irwin.

U.S. Department of Commerce. (1998). "Statistical Abstract of the United States." Washington, DC.: U.S. Government Printing Office.

Voth, E.R. & Myers, R. (1993). *The New Owner: Making the Transition from Employee to Employer*. Homewood, IL: Business One Irwin.

Walstad, W.B. (ed.). (1994). *An International Perspective on Economic Education*. Boston, MA: Kluwer Academic Publishers.

Walstad, W.B. (1998). "Why It's Important to Understand Economics," *The Region* (Federal Reserve Bank of Minneapolis), 12(4), 23-26.

Walstad, W.B. & Kourilsky, M.L. (1998). "Entrepreneurial Attitudes and Knowledge of Black Youth," *Entrepreneurship Theory and Practice*, 23(2), 5-18.

Walstad, W.B. & Kourilsky, M.L. (1999). *Seeds of Success: Entrepreneurship and Youth*. Dubuque, IA: Kendall/Hunt Publishing.

Walstad, W.B. & Rebeck, K. (1999). "How Does Economic Education Impact Economic Literacy?", *The Region* (Federal Reserve Bank of Minneapolis), 13(2), 18-21.

Walstad, W.B. & Rebeck, K. (2000). "The Status of Economics in The High School Curriculum," *Journal of Economic Education*, 31(1), 95-101.

Williams, G. (1999). "2001: An Entrepreneurial Odyssey," *Entrepreneur*, 27(4) (April), 106-113.

Van der Kuip, I. (1998). *Early Development of Entrepreneurial Qualities*. Strategic Study. Zoertermeer, The Netherlands: EIM.

Young, J.E. (1997). "Entrepreneurship Education and Learning for University Students and Practicing Entrepreneurs." In D. Sexton and R. Smilor (eds.), *Entrepreneurship 2000*, (pp. 215-238). Chicago, IL: Upstart Publishing.